The
ANTIQUES
ROADSHOW
A celebration of the first 21 years

The ANTIQUES ROADSHOW

A celebration of the first 21 years

Fiona Malcolm

SPECIAL CONSULTANT Paul Atterbury

FOREWORD BY Hugh Scully

MITCHELL BEAZLEY

The Antiques Roadshow: A celebration of the first 21 years

First published in Great Britain in 1998
by Mitchell Beazley, an imprint of
Reed Consumer Books Limited,
Michelin House, 81 Fulham Road,
London SW3 6RB

By arrangement with the BBC.
Based on the BBC Television Programme.
'Antiques Roadshow' is a trademark of the
British Broadcasting Corporation and used under licence.
Antiques Roadshow logo © BBC 1989.

Executive Editor **Alison Starling**
Executive Art Editor **Vivienne Brar**
Designer **Dan Newman**
Senior Editor **Anthea Snow**
Editor **Richard Dawes**
Editorial Assistant **Stephen Guise**
Picture Research **Claire Gouldstone**
Production **Rachel Staveley**
Special photography **Tim Ridley, Nick Goodall, Ron Sutherland**
Index **Ann Barrett**

ISBN 1 84000 072 4

A CIP record for this book is available from the British Library

Set in Berkeley and Syntax
Produced by Toppan Printing Co., Ltd
Printed and bound in China

Page 1: Ozzy the Owl, a Staffordshire
slipware drinking pot (c.1685–90) found in
Northampton in 1989. Valued at over
£20,000, it would now be worth £30–40,000.
(See page 103)

Page 2: An overhead shot on the day of the
Antiques Roadshow. Visitors patiently queue
while the portable single camera ('PSC')
moves about the hall.

Page 5: *Sinews of Old England* by
George Elgar Hicks (1824–1914) found in
Stoke-on-Trent in 1993. Bought for £55 in
the mid-1960s, it was valued at £25,000 on
the *Roadshow.*

Contents

FOREWORD by Hugh Scully 6

HOW THE PROGRAMME STARTED 8

    The birth of an idea 10

    The locations 12

THE TEAM 16

    The presenters 18

    The experts 20

MAKING THE PROGRAMME 48

    Planning the Roadshows 50

    Setting up at the location 52

    Hugh Scully's introduction 56

    The furniture round 58

    On the day 62

    Editing for broadcast 72

    Overseas Roadshows 74

    The Next Generation 78

    An overwhelming response… 82

THE GREAT FINDS 86

    Favourite treasures 138

    The new collectables 146

GLOSSARY 148

INDEX 150

ACKNOWLEDGEMENTS 152

Foreword by Hugh Scully

The *Antiques Roadshow* is a unique phenomenon in British broadcasting. No-one predicted that a programme about art and antiques could ever appeal to a regular audience of many millions. It is television's most unexpected success. Certainly none of us who take part in the programme today ever imagined in those early years that we would still be together to celebrate our 21st birthday. The obvious question is: 'Why?' What is it that has made the *Antiques Roadshow* one of BBC Television's longest-running hits?

The answer is to be found in the patient queues of people who flock to each location when the *Roadshow* comes to town. Every programme is a cameo of the British character: its foibles, idiosyncrasies and eccentricities. More recently, the shows recorded abroad have reflected the characters and cultures of other nations.

In a later chapter you will be able to read about some of our great finds, but, breathtaking as they are, it is often the people themselves that we most readily remember. They *are* the *Antiques Roadshow*. They give it the colour, charm, interest, anecdote and humour that delight us on Sunday evenings. We enjoy their happiness. We share their hopes. We feel their disappointments, and they leave their marks on our memories. I still vividly recall many of the *Roadshow's* characters. There was the lady in Bognor Regis who arrived at midday in evening dress, believing that she should dress appropriately for her appearance in 'an evening programme'. I remember too the young man in crash helmet and motorcycle leathers who roared up at Leamington Spa with a fabulous collection of Russian silver in a simple cardboard box tied, rather insecurely, to the pillion. Having had his Tsarist silver valued in thousands he disappeared, as he had arrived, in a puff of smoke. In Exeter another lady threw her valueless picture over the nearest hedge as she left, and a man who had just been given a valuation was found queuing to see another expert for 'a second opinion'.

The other reason for the success of the show is, of course, the experts. Even after many years in their company I never cease to be amazed by the depth of their knowledge and the relaxed and friendly way in which they explain the complexities of a 19th-century French clock, or the tell-tale signs of a faked picture. David Battie, one of our pottery and porcelain experts, says that he has to be able to recognize two hundred different shades of white. Few of us will ever possess such extraordinary knowledge or insight, but on the *Roadshow* this great expertise is available each week to entertain and educate us.

The final element in the complex operation that brings the *Roadshow* to your screen is the highly skilled production team working under executive producer Christopher Lewis. In these pages you will meet many of those who are constantly busy behind the scenes and whose individual talents are so essential to the smooth running of the show. If the *Antiques Roadshow* appears to glide along like a graceful maiden aunt, it is only because a well honed team of professional people are working very hard to make that vision seem so effortless. With the publication of this book the maiden aunt reaches the age of 21. Perhaps she has a few more years yet.

Miscellaneous

◀ Angela Rippon and Arthur Negus discuss the day's events with an expert and a customer at the Trowbridge *Roadshow*, **which was filmed for the second series.**

How the programme started

Those who were involved in the first *Antiques Roadshow*, which took place on 17 May 1977 at the Town Hall in Hereford, had no inkling that before long it would become compulsive viewing for millions. Today, far from having run its course, the programme is not only a British institution, but also the largest regular public event put on by the BBC. Over the years the *Roadshow* has reached every corner of the British Isles and beyond, each event bringing together a world-class team of experts to share their knowledge with a patient public prepared to wait hours to learn more about their treasures. It is a winning formula, guaranteed to give pleasure to viewers for years to come.

The birth of an idea

Like most great ideas, the concept of the *Antiques Roadshow* is such an obviously good one that it seems hard to imagine a time when it was not an essential part of Sunday afternoon for millions of viewers. And, as with other events that have become institutions, many of the people who took part in the first series feel justifiably proud to have been part of the programme's early development.

To trace the *Roadshow's* real origins we have to look back further than 1977, which is when the first *Roadshow* was filmed, to the late 1960s, when *Going for a Song* was in full swing. It was joined in the 1970s by *Collectors' World*, which was also produced by BBC Bristol.

Watched every week by a growing number of devoted viewers, *Going for a Song* starred one Arthur Negus as the accessible face of antiques collecting. Plucked from the Gloucester auctioneers Bruton Knowles in 1965, at the age of 65, with no previous experience of television, he was soon to become a household name.

Arthur's friendly approach on *Going for a Song*, and the weekly broadcast competitions and the question-and-answer sessions on *Collectors' World*, were generating sackloads of post. There was clearly a colossal interest in antiques on the part of the public, and viewers were bursting with questions about what they hoped were their treasures. Who made them, when and where – and, of course, how much were they worth?

In 1976 the executives of BBC Bristol's General Programmes Unit commissioned a report on what was currently being done in the world of programmes on antiques, and what direction these should be taking in the future. After a good deal of discussion it was agreed that a format whereby members of the public brought along their own objects to show to a team of experts would stand a very good chance of being a success. At the very least, it would certainly fill the gap more satisfactorily than answering letters of enquiry ever could.

Several people from BBC Bristol went to Tavistock, in Devon, to watch Sotheby's staff at work during a valuation day. For many years the major auction houses have used these days (also known as 'open days' or 'sweeps') in order to encourage the public to bring along their antiques for a free valuation – in the hope, of course, that it would generate business.

The new show developed along similar lines, but with an important difference: the *Roadshow* would be a public event with no commercial agenda. The experts would dispense their knowledge, but not their business cards.

Every new series starts life with a pilot programme, to test its potential, and Hereford Town Hall was picked as the ideal venue for the *Antiques Roadshow's* trial run. Hereford was a prosperous market town a comfortable distance from Bristol for the outside broadcast unit to travel, and situated not too far from the densely populated Midlands. The event was advertised in advance, and people

▲ A young Hugo Morley-Fletcher and Arthur Negus, by then the elder statesman of antiques programmes, discuss an object at one of the early *Roadshows*.

were asked to contact BBC Bristol if they had large pieces of furniture or paintings which they themselves could not bring in on the day.

The pilot took place in an upstairs hall on a much smaller scale than viewers are used to today, but had basically the same format. Someone took an initial look at customers' offerings before directing them to the appropriate experts. The customers were not fitted with microphones before an item was recorded, as they are today, and no-one worried about the cameras intruding into shot while they roamed around the room – a very innovative approach at the time.

At the end of that first gathering the executive producer, the late Robin Drake, called the experts together to discuss the day's events and the objects they had seen. What would the managers think of the footage? the team wondered. They need not have been concerned, for they had set in motion one of the great success stories of British television.

▲ A walnut spinet made in 1730. It has its original brass hinges, and ivory and ebony keys with pressed paper patterns at the ends. Valued at £10–20,000 in 1990.

▼ A set of four 'Street Cries of London' silver salts made by the famous London firm of Hunt, Storr and Mortimer. Valued at £20,000 in 1997.

▲ A rare Japanese Kakiemon vase made 1660–70 and exported to the west not long after Japanese porcelain decorators began to add yellow to their palette of colours. Valued at £9–12,000 in 1995.

◄ A fine porcelain plaque made in Berlin and painted in Vienna in 1880. Young girls with flowing locks are much sought-after as subject matter. Valued at £15–20,000 in 1990.

The locations

Series One: 1977 and 1978

Location	Venue	Recorded
Hereford	Town Hall	17 May 1977
(pilot programme)		
Bedworth	Civic Centre	26 April 1978
Yeovil	Johnson Hall	17 May 1978
Newbury	Newbury Corn Exchange	7 June 1978
Northallerton	Hambleton Civic Hall	5 July 1978
Buxton	Buxton Pavilion	19 July 1978
Perth	Town Hall	28 July 1978
Mold	Theatr Clwyd Complex	23 August 1978

Series Two: 1979

Location	Venue	Recorded
Trowbridge	Civic Hall	28 June 1979
Llandridnod Wells	Grand Pavilion	17 July 1979
Ely	The Maltings	2 August 1979
Oldham	Civic Centre	14 August 1979
Maidstone	College of Further and Higher Education	30 August 1979
Camberley	Civic Hall	21 September 1979
Stoke-on-Trent	Kings Hall, Kingsway	11 October 1979
St Peter Port, Guernsey	The Beau Séjour Leisure Centre	18 October 1979

Series Three: 1980

Location	Venue	Recorded
Salisbury	City Hall	15 May 1980
Monmouth	Monmouth Leisure Centre	29 May 1980
Cheltenham	Town Hall	12 June 1980
Troon	The Concert Hall	3 July 1980
Aylesbury	Civic Centre	28 August 1980
Aberystwyth	The Great Hall, The Arts Centre	25 September 1980
Derby	The Great Hall, The Assembly Rooms	9 October 1980
Bognor Regis	The Bognor Regis Centre	23 October 1980

Series Four: 1981

Location	Venue	Recorded
St Austell	Cornwall Coliseum	20 May 1981
Lancaster	Town Hall	4 June 1981
Winchester	The Guildhall	17 June 1981

Leamington Spa	Royal Spa Centre	2 July 1981
Bolton	The Albert Hall	16 July 1981
Exeter	The Great Hall, Exeter University	3 September 1981
Scarborough	Spa Grand Hall	14 October 1981
Malvern	The Winter Gardens	4 November 1981

Series Five: 1982

Location	Venue	Recorded
Gloucester	Gloucester Leisure Centre	16 June 1982
Harrogate	Royal Baths Assembly Rooms	8 July 1982
Dundee	The Caird Hall	22 July 1982
Leicester	De Montfort Hall	8 September 1982
Torquay	Town Hall	22 September 1982
Norwich	St Andrew's and Blackfriars' Hall	30 September 1982
Southport	The Floral Hall	20 October 1982
Folkestone	The Leas Cliff Hall	3 November 1982

Series Six: 1983

Location	Venue	Recorded
St Helier, Jersey	Gloucester Hall	28 March 1983
Poole	Poole Arts Centre	9 June 1983
Crewe	The Oakley Centre	27 July 1983
Reading	The Hexagon	7 September 1983
Aberdeen	The Music Hall	21 September 1983
Eastbourne	The Winter Garden	5 October 1983
Blackburn	King George's Hall	19 October 1983

Series Seven: 1984

Location	Venue	Recorded
Plymouth	The Guildhall	7 June 1984
Kendal	South Lakeland Leisure Centre	21 June 1984
Banbury	Spiceball Park Leisure Centre	5 July 1984
Nottingham	Sports Centre, University of Nottingham	19 July 1984
Swansea	The Brangwyn Hall, The Guildhall	6 September 1984
Sunderland	Crowtree Leisure Centre	13 September 1984
Portsmouth	The Guildhall	11 October 1984
Douglas, Isle of Man	Villa Marina	25 October 1984

Series Eight: 1985

Location	Venue	Recorded
Wolverhampton	Civic Hall	6 June 1985
Edinburgh	Meadowbank Sports Centre	27 June 1985
Ipswich	The Corn Exchange	11 July 1985
Bedford	The Bunyan Centre	25 July 1985
Llandudno	Canolfan Aberconwy Centre	5 September 1985
Doncaster	Exhibition Centre, Doncaster Racecourse	26 September 1985
Hull	City Hall	3 October 1985
Swindon	Oasis Leisure Centre	17 October 1985
Watford	Town Hall	25 October 1985
Southend-on-Sea	Cliffs Pavilion	7 November 1985

Series Nine: 1986

Location	Venue	Recorded
Barnstaple	North Devon Leisure Centre	15 May 1986
Dunfermline	The Glen Pavilion	29 May 1986
Southampton	The Guildhall	12 June 1986
Chester	Northgate Arena	26 June 1986
Bath	Leisure Centre, North Parade	3 July 1986
Newcastle upon Tyne	Eldon Square Recreation Centre	17 July 1986
Preston	The Guildhall	4 September 1986
Carlisle	The Sands Centre	18 September 1986
Worthing	The Assembly Hall	2 October 1986
Peterborough	The Wirrina Stadium	16 October 1986
Camborne	Carn Brea Leisure Centre	30 October 1986
Margate	The Winter Gardens	7 November 1986

Series Ten: 1987

Location	Venue	Recorded
Worcester	Perdiswell Sports Centre	6 May 1987
Great Yarmouth	Marina Leisure Centre	21 May 1987
Chelmsford	Riverside Leisure Centre	25 June 1987
Cambridge	Corn Exchange	9 July 1987
Glasgow	The Scottish Exhibition and Conference Centre	23 July 1987
Cardiff	St David's Hall	3 September 1987
Bradford	Richard Dunn Sports Centre	17 September 1987
Middlesbrough	Rainbow Leisure Centre	1 October 1987
Ventnor, Isle of Wight	Winter Gardens	8 October 1987
Belfast, N Ireland	Ulster Hall	22 October 1987
Maidenhead	Magnet Leisure Centre	29 October 1987
Sheffield	Cutlers' Hall	11 November 1987

Series Eleven: 1988

Location	Venue	Recorded
Liverpool	St George's Hall	28 April 1988
Harrow	Harrow Leisure Centre	12 May 1988
Birmingham	Cocks Moor Leisure Centre	26 May 1988
Bournemouth	Bournemouth International Conference Centre	16 June 1988
Bristol	Brunel Centre	23 June 1988
Dublin, Ireland	The Royal Hospital, Kilmainham	7 July 1988
Guildford	Civic Hall	21 July 1988
Leeds	Sports Centre, University of Leeds	8 September 1988
Newark-on-Trent	Kelham Hall	22 September 1988
Hastings	Hastings Sports Centre	5 October 1988
Glenrothes	Fife Sports Centre	20 October 1988
Tavistock	Tavistock Pannier Market	2 November 1988

Series Twelve: 1989

Location	Venue	Recorded
Blackpool	Tower Ballroom	12 April 1989
Manchester	Town Hall	27 April 1989
Lincoln	Lincoln Cathedral	25 May 1989
Helsingor, Denmark	Elsinore Castle	31 May 1989
Malmö, Sweden	Masshallarna	4 June 1989
Elgin	The High School	6 July 1989
Leominster	Leominster Leisure Centre	20 July 1989
Northampton	Derngate Centre	7 September 1989
Paignton	Torbay Leisure Centre	14 September 1989
Tunbridge Wells	The Assembly Hall	28 September 1989
Hornchurch	Hornchurch Sports Centre	5 October 1989
Brighton	The Corn Exchange	26 October 1989

Series Thirteen: 1990

Location	Venue	Recorded
Darlington	The Dolphin Centre	26 April 1990
Merthyr Tydfil	Rhydcar Leisure Centre	3 May 1990
Stowmarket	Mid-Suffolk Leisure Centre	24 May 1990
London	The Business Design Centre, Islington	14 June 1990
Hexham	Wentworth Leisure Centre	28 June 1990
Whitehaven	Whitehaven Sports Centre	12 July 1990
Ayr	Dam Park Hall	26 July 1990
Salisbury	Salisbury Cathedral	6 September 1990
St Ives	St Ives Recreation Centre	20 September 1990

Stafford ....Stychfields Hall...................4 October 1990
Gillingham ....St George's Conference ....18 October 1990
Centre
Valletta, Malta..............Mediterranean ....3 November 1990
Conference Centre

Series Fourteen: 1991

Location	Venue	Recorded
Queensferry	Deeside Leisure Centre	2 May 1991
Cleethorpes	Cleethorpes Leisure Centre	16 May 1991
London	Alexandra Palace	30 May 1991
Farnham	Farnham Sports Centre	13 June 1991
Enniskillen, N Ireland	The Lakeland Forum	27 June 1991
Chippenham	The Olympiad Leisure Centre	11 July 1991
Stratford-upon-Avon	Civic Hall	5 September 1991
Yeovilton	Fleet Air Arm Museum	19 September 1991
York	The Barbican	3 October 1991
Hemel Hempstead	The Dacorum Pavilion	17 October 1991
Stromness, Orkney	Stromness Academy	27 October 1991
Rochdale	Town Hall	14 November 1991
Bristol	Brunel Centre	24 November 1991

(The Next Generation)

Series Fifteen: 1992

Location	Venue	Recorded
Spalding	Castle Sports Complex	7 May 1992
Chesterfield	Queens Park Sports Centre	21 May 1992
Berwick-Upon-Tweed	Bonarsteads Leisure Centre	4 June 1992
Aberdeen	Exhibition and Conference Centre, Bridge of Don	2 July 1992
Macclesfield	Macclesfield Leisure Centre	16 July 1992
Kingsbridge	Kingsbridge Sports Centre	30 July 1992
Kingston, Jamaica	Devon House	6 September 1992
Coventry	Warwick University Arts Centre	17 September 1992
London	Kensington Town Hall	8 October 1992
Beaulieu	National Motor Museum	15 October 1992
Pembroke	Pembroke Leisure Centre	29 October 1992
Arundel	Baron's Hall, Arundel Castle	12 November 1992
York	National Railway Museum	22 November 1992

(The Next Generation)

Series Sixteen: 1993

Location	Venue	Recorded
Stoke-on-Trent	The Grand Hall, Trentham Gardens	13 May 1993
Kidderminster	Forest Glades Leisure Centre	27 May 1993

Cork, Ireland	City Hall	7 June 1993
Beaumaris, Anglesey	Canolfan Beaumaris Leisure Centre	24 June 1993
Exeter	The Great Hall, Exeter University	8 July 1993
Barrow-in-Furness	Park Leisure Centre	15 July 1993
Suffolk	Hevingham Hall	29 July 1993
London	Olympia Exhibition Centre	11 September 1993
Crawley	The Hawth Theatre	16 September 1993
Ashford	The Stour Centre	30 September 1993
County Durham	Raby Castle	14 October 1993
Motherwell	Motherwell Concert Hall	21 October 1993
King's Lynn	Lynnsport and Leisure Park	28 October 1993
Gibraltar	Central Hall	11 November 1993
London	Science Museum	28 November 1993

(The Next Generation)

Series Seventeen: 1994

Location	Venue	Recorded
Truro	Truro Cathedral	23 June 1994
Colchester	Charter Hall, Leisure World	5 May 1994
Wellington	Wrekin College	19 May 1994
Bridlington	The Spa Royal Hotel	2 June 1994
Bexhill-on-Sea	De La Warr Pavilion	14 June 1994
Inverness	Inverness Sports Centre	7 July 1994
Bedfordshire	Luton Hoo	21 July 1994
Basingstoke	The Anvil	28 July 1994
Derby	Assembly Rooms	8 September 1994
St Peter Port, Guernsey	The Beau Séjour Leisure Centre	22 September 1994
Newcastle Emlyn	Newcastle Emlyn Leisure Centre	29 September 1994
Huddersfield	Huddersfield Sports Centre	13 October 1994
Taunton	Blackbrook Pavilion	20 October 1994
Oxfordshire	Blenheim Palace	3 November 1994
London	Granada Studios Tour	19 November 1994

(The Next Generation)

Brussels, Belgium	Salle de la Madeleine	21 February 1995
Accrington	Hyndburn Sports Centre	2 March 1995
Wymondham	Wymondham Leisure Centre	9 March 1995

Series Eighteen: 1995

Location	Venue	Recorded
Ely	Ely Cathedral	4 May 1995
Dover	Dover Leisure Centre	18 May 1995
Llangollen	Royal International Pavilion	1 June 1995

Location	Venue	Recorded
St Helier, Jersey	Fort Regent Leisure Centre	8 June 1995
Stirling	University of Stirling Sports Centre	22 June 1995
Alnwick	Alnwick Castle	6 July 1995
Henley	Henley Management College	23 July 1995
Cheltenham	Town Hall	27 July 1995
Weymouth	Weymouth Sports Centre	7 September 1995
North Yorkshire	Fountains Abbey	13 September 1995
Peebles	Gytes Leisure Centre	12 October 1995
Penarth	Penarth Leisure Centre	19 October 1995
Windermere	The Lakes School	2 November 1995
Mansfield	Mansfield Leisure Centre	9 November 1995
Belfast, N Ireland (The Next Generation)	Ulster Folk and Transport Museum	19 November 1995
Amsterdam, Netherlands	St Olof's Chapel, Golden Tulip Barbizon Palace Hotel	25 February 1996
Broxbourne	Civic Centre	7 March 1996

Series Nineteen: 1996

Location	Venue	Recorded
Ludlow	South Shropshire Leisure Centre	25 April 1996
Portsmouth	Historic Dockyard Boathouse No 7	2 May 1996
Market Harborough	Harborough Leisure Centre	16 May 1996
Chepstow	Chepstow Leisure and Education Centre	30 May 1996
Cornwall	Lanhydrock	7 June 1996
Penzance / Isles of Scilly	St John's Hall, Penzance	11 June 1996
Derbyshire	Chatsworth	27 June 1996
Perth	City Halls	10 July 1996
Portree, Skye	Portree Community Centre	13 July 1996
Lyme Regis	Allhallows College	18 July 1996
East Sussex	Michelham Priory	25 July 1996
Horsham	Christ's Hospital, The Bluecoat School	5 September 1996
Buckinghamshire	Waddesdon Manor	19 September 1996
London	The Indoor School, Lord's Cricket Ground	26 September 1996
The Wirral	The Oval Leisure Centre	3 October 1996
Skegness	The Embassy Centre	10 October 1996
Pickering	North Ryedale Leisure Centre	24 October 1996
Aberystwyth	Plascrug Leisure Centre	31 October 1996
Saffron Walden	Lord Butler Leisure Centre	7 November 1996
Edinburgh (The Next Generation)	Royal Museum of Scotland	17 November 1996
Arras, France	Hôtel de Ville	15 February 1997
Moreton-in-Marsh	Fire Service College	21 February 1997

Series Twenty: 1997

Location	Venue	Recorded
Barnsley	Metrodome Centre	16 April 1997
Fort William	Marco's An Aird Leisure Centre	24 April 1997
Woking	Woking Leisure Centre	8 May 1997
Altrincham	Altrincham Leisure Centre	15 May 1997
Walsall	Town Hall	29 May 1997
Minehead	Minehead Station	11 June 1997
Lincolnshire	Burghley House	19 June 1997
Norfolk	Blickling Hall	25 June 1997
Marlborough	Marlborough College	10 July 1997
St David's	Bishop's Palace	16 July 1997
Oxford	Christ Church College	24 July 1997

Location	Venue	Recorded
West Dean	West Dean College	4 September 1997
Dartmouth	Britannia Royal Naval College	11 September 1997
Durham	Abbey Sports Centre	18 September 1997
Hull	City Hall	2 October 1997
Newport, Isle of Wight	Medina Centre	9 October 1997
Weston-super-Mare	RAF Locking	23 October 1997
Porthmadog	Porthmadog Leisure Centre	30 October 1997
Bolton	Bolton Wanderers Football Stadium	6 November 1997
Cardiff (The Next Generation)	Techniquest	16 November 1997
County Clare, Ireland	Dromoland Castle	27 November 1997
Brecon	Brecon Leisure Centre	5 March 1998
Canterbury	Kingsmead Leisure Centre	12 March 1998
Cannock	Chase Leisure Centre	19 March 1998

Series Twenty-one: 1998

Location	Venue	Recorded
Bletchley	Bletchley Leisure Centre	23 April 1998
Welshpool	Welshpool Leisure Centre	30 April 1998
Stranraer	Ryan Centre	7 May 1998
London	Syon Park	21 May 1998
Tetbury	Westonbirt School	28 May 1998
Suffolk	Ickworth House	4 June 1998
Cheshire	Lyme Park	18 June 1998
Poole	Poole Arts Centre	25 June 1998
Berkshire	Highclere Castle	9 July 1998
Colwyn Bay	Colwyn Bay Leisure Centre	16 July 1998
Ormskirk	Edge Hill University College	23 July 1998
Dorking	Dorking Halls	30 July 1998
London	Greenwich Royal Naval College	3 September 1998
Gainsborough	West Lindsey Leisure Centre	10 September 1998
Plymouth	The Guildhall	17 September 1998
Carnoustie	Carnoustie Leisure Centre	1 October 1998
Gateshead	Gateshead International Stadium	8 October 1998
Northallerton	Hambleton Leisure Centre	15 October 1998
Shoreham-by-Sea	Lancing College	29 October 1998

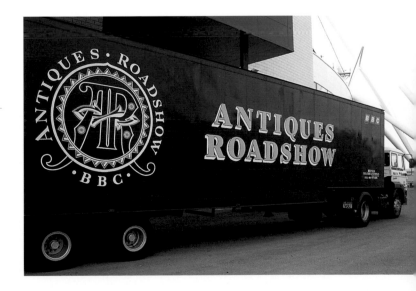

The team

◀ Members of the team assemble with Hugh Scully in the moments before they take their places and welcome the public at the start of another *Roadshow*.

At every *Roadshow* a team of around 21 experts arrives on site by 9.30 in the morning, ready to answer the questions and solve the puzzles posed during a day when each of them might look at up to a thousand objects. The full roster of close to 80 experts is mixed and matched in rotation from a rich pool of auction-house specialists, dealers, lecturers, museum curators and writers, so that a good balance and breadth of knowledge can be drawn on at every event.

The rapidly shifting and changing field of collecting is reflected in a team that is constantly revised, allowing fresh ideas and faces to mingle with those familiar and well-loved characters who have graced our screens for many years.

The presenters

Bruce Parker was asked to present the first series of the *Antiques Roadshow* by its executive producer, the late Robin Drake. 'I remember the whole experience as tremendous fun,' says Bruce, who is still a familiar face on BBC television, presenting *South Today* as well as his own weekly political commentary programme, *South of Westminster*, from Southampton. 'The most extraordinary thing about it as far as I was concerned was how many people turned up during the filming of the entire first series, despite the fact that it didn't get transmitted until some months later.'

He also remembers being struck by the amount of knowledge accumulated in such a short time by the very young team of experts who arrived to take their seats during that first ground-breaking series. 'There were people like Hugo Morley Fletcher, David Battie, Simon Bull and a young chap who was a paintings expert and mad about Chelsea Football Club.' He is referring, of course, to Philip Hook, still a Chelsea fan after all these years. 'They all knew so much about their subjects that I felt quite humbled.'

Bruce recalls the time the *Roadshow* team was walking through Hereford with Arthur Negus on the day before the pilot programme was filmed. Suddenly a van screeched to a halt beside them, the driver leapt out, opened up the back, pulled out an antique chair and asked Arthur to value it on the spot. 'We couldn't believe it,' says Bruce. 'The posters were up in the town, but we could never work out how he managed to track us down at that particular moment with the chair conveniently in the back of his van. Arthur loved the public, so it didn't bother him one bit, but it was a bizarre encounter!'

Series two and three were presented by Angela Rippon, who was also mesmerized by the combined talents of the experts. 'I used to sit at the tables to listen to them and was always bowled over by what they knew – and in such depth!' She also has fond memories of executive producer Robin Drake: 'He was such a wonderful man and cared so much about the programme. He took great trouble over every tiny detail, which is what has always made it such a successful public event.'

The *Roadshow* gave the public an unprecedented insight into the process of making a television programme. 'It has become so much more commonplace now,' Angela continues, 'but at the beginning of the 1980s it was the best opportunity people had to come along and watch how it was done. They could stand around the main unit and see the

▲ Bruce Parker, the presenter of the first series of the *Antiques Roadshow* when it was broadcast in 1978, still works for the BBC in Southampton.

▲ Angela Rippon, the presenter of the second and third series, sits at an expert's table to admire an object brought in by a visitor to the *Roadshow*.

◀ Hugh Scully (left), not long after he took over as presenter of the *Antiques Roadshow* for the fourth series, seen here with Arthur Negus.

▼ Hugh Scully admires a Chinese vase against an impressive backdrop at one of the *Roadshow*'s cathedral locations.

time as well as the skill and care that went into recording every item. I think the programme has been a marvellous exercise in public relations for the BBC, because people could see what they were getting for their licence fee.'

When Angela left to join TV-AM, Hugh Scully was invited to become presenter. He has been with the programme ever since, combining the demands of constant travelling with, first, presenting *Nationwide* and then running his own production company. He joined the *Roadshow* in 1981 for series four, but already had a track record of presenting antiques programmes that dated back to the 1960s.

'The story starts in 1966, which was the year my wife Barbara and I married,' Hugh explains. 'We furnished our first house in Devon on £500 with Victorian pieces bought at country auctions. A BBC producer came to supper one evening and admired our antiques. Then, two years later, he rang me and asked me to chair the Radio 4 programme *Talking about Antiques*. I went on to present *Collectors' World* on BBC2, which ran for several years, before joining the *Roadshow*.'

The format of the programme and the style of presentation have remained almost unchanged over the years. 'It has retained its freshness without having to make any drastic changes, purely because of the unpredictable nature of the event,' says Hugh. 'You never know what you are going to find.' Hugh also points out that it is highly unusual for pilot programmes – which are made to test new ideas – to be transmitted, but in this case the very first event at Hereford Town Hall was such an instant success with the powers that be that it was included in the first series.

'It was an obviously winning formula, right from the beginning,' says Hugh. 'But, having said that, no-one who was involved in those days dreamt that it would go on captivating audiences for as long as it has.' The public is the secret of the *Roadshow*'s success, he insists. 'I've always maintained that the programme is about people, their background and sense of humour, how they came to own their objects – and even their mild eccentricity. The only guarantee at any event is that you come away at the end of the day with 45 minutes' worth of splendid television.'

The experts

Becoming a *Roadshow* expert involves jumping through a daunting series of hoops before eventual acceptance as part of the 'family'. Generally word of mouth starts the ball rolling. 'We're always on the lookout for fresh blood, particularly women experts and younger faces,' says executive producer Christopher Lewis. 'Once someone has been suggested to us we arrange to meet them and, if that goes well, invite them to a *Roadshow* to observe. They sit at the table with the other experts and deal with the public, but I keep a close eye on how they cope with the volume and the range of things put in front of them.'

The depth and range of each expert's knowledge is vital to the success of the day, as is the way in which they complement one another. 'We must have the very best in the room at every *Roadshow* because we so often get the very best objects coming through the door,' Christopher explains. 'They need to work as a team and be able to consult each other, so we are careful to choose a good mix each time.

'It would not be a good idea, for instance, if both picture experts on any one day were specialists in Old Masters. They have to be able to deal with anything that turns up. Similarly, we need people on the Miscellaneous tables who can deal with toys and dolls as well as scientific instruments, textiles and plastics. Good generalists are very valuable to us.'

When an important object has been booked into the recording schedule, the expert often needs to do research with his or her colleagues. 'Their range of contacts becomes vital,' says Christopher. 'The fact that they probably know the world's leading experts in any field means they have access to the best and most reliable information available.'

They must also act as representatives of the BBC for the day, enjoy working with the public and be able to deal with the stress of performing in front of the camera. 'Recording can be very intimidating for new people. We understand that and feed

▲ Miscellaneous expert Graham Lay puts his mind to solving the mystery of a 'baby' violin.

them in gradually. It can take years for an expert to speak naturally and fluently with the customer and make him or her feel at ease. It is unlike any other television situation they might find themselves in, because they have to be both expert and interviewer, and that requires a high level of professionalism, for which they have not been trained.'

Christopher attempts to alleviate any anxieties by presenting each new recruit

with a document on how to handle objects and talk to customers in front of the camera. He has also initiated occasional training days, when the participants act as director, camera operator and stage manager rolled into one: 'It helps them to understand the process from every angle, and has proved very successful.'

Marc Allum miscellaneous

Marc began collecting as a small boy and later, while studying for a degree in English and Media Studies, supplemented his student income by buying and selling at auction. He then trained as a sound engineer, but, deciding he had made the wrong career choice, became an independent dealer again for two years before joining Rosebery's, the south London auctioneers, nine years ago. A generalist, Marc has responsibility for works of art and collectors' items, including toys and scientific instruments. His pride and joy are his 1960 Cadillac and early-19th-century house, which absorb all of his spare time. Marc joined the *Roadshow* team in 1998.

George Archdale miscellaneous

George has worked in the antiques business for over 20 years, training first at Sotheby's and then working for Bonhams before spending five years as an independent dealer in the north of England. He has also been an antiques consultant in the insurance world and spent a year working on *Miller's Antiques Price Guide*. He was a regional representative for Sotheby's for ten years before moving to Vosts' Fine Art Auctioneers in Newmarket; he has recently joined Dreweatt Neate in Newbury. When not taking care of clients' interests, George scours the local woods for wild mushrooms with his faithful Jack Russell terrier.

John Axford pottery and porcelain

John studied Fine Arts at Leeds University before joining Phillips to work as an administrator, which whetted his appetite for the world of antiques and auction houses. He went to the Southampton Institute and completed the two-year course for valuers and auctioneers, gaining the highest marks for valuations and winning the Ivor Turnbull Memorial Prize. John is now Head of the Ceramics and Glass Department at the auctioneers Woolley & Wallis, in Salisbury, and lectures regularly at the Southampton Institute. He first appeared on the *Antiques Roadshow* in 1998.

Jon Baddeley miscellaneous

Jon read Engineering at university and began working as a porter at Sotheby's as a vacation job. Finding that many of his colleagues were arts-based and that he had a natural affinity with objects such as typewriters and clockwork toys, which people were beginning to collect in the early 1970s, he started the Collectors' Department in 1974 and is now Head of the Collectors' Division. Jon's own passion is for folk art, especially naïve sailor work, and he is the author, for Sotheby's publications, of *Nautical Antiques and Collectables*.

Paul Atterbury miscellaneous see page 22

Paul Atterbury

◀ Paul sits in an oak armchair designed by Robert 'Mouseman' Thompson (note the mouse carved in relief on the left leg). He is holding a Poole Pottery plate made in 1935, with a design showing a trawler called *Polly*, which is also the name of Paul's elder daughter. On his left is a 1950s coffee table with a Formica top decorated in the manner of John Piper. The Gitanes ashtray symbolizes Paul's belief in individual freedom, including the right to smoke. On the wall behind is a close-up of a battleship painted c.1944, which is unsigned but is typical of the work of many war artists. Next to it hangs a painting – in the style of Lowry – of Stoke-on-Trent, where Paul lived for a while. Below is a 1930s Heal's bureau bookcase laden with some of his favourite pieces. Top, left to right: a Sèvres vase (1934), painted with an industrial scene by G Guer; three Doulton Lambeth stoneware sculptures; a Dutch Permurende Art Nouveau vase; and an orange polar bear by Minton (1905). Bottom: a 1950s Andy Pandy mug, a memento of Paul's mother, the puppeteer who operated Andy Pandy on BBC children's television; a modern primitive-style ship made by an artist in Cornwall; and a Moorcroft polar bear vase designed by Sally Tuffin in 1987.

The colourful assortment of objects with which Paul has chosen to furnish and decorate his comfortable, unpretentious home is a good clue to the breadth of his interests. Visitors to the *Roadshow* can always rely on his knowing at least half-a-dozen useful and fascinating facts about almost anything put in front of him.

Paul began to soak up this knowledge during childhood. Both his parents were keen collectors, inspiring similar interests in their son. After leaving school, he trained as a graphic designer and then took a degree in Art History at the University of East Anglia before embarking on a succession of careers that enabled him to transform his passions into his livelihood.

It was while he was working for a firm of publishers during the mid-1960s that Paul began buying English art pottery. At this time it was still possible to pick up examples of Moorcroft at antiques markets for £5–10 apiece. He now also

began to write and lecture about ceramics, and as a result of these activities spent four years as Historical Adviser to Royal Doulton in Stoke-on-Trent.

Paul was editor of *The Connoisseur* magazine between 1980 and 1981, and has since pursued a career as a writer and lecturer, often appearing on television. In 1994 he was Curator of the major Pugin exhibition at the Victoria and Albert Museum, bringing together important pieces by the great Victorian architect and designer Augustus Welby Northmore Pugin, assembled from churches and art collections all over Britain.

▶ A silver covered dish designed by H G Murphy in 1934. Murphy was the leading English craft silversmith of the Art Deco period, a time when English craftsmen were often overshadowed by their European contemporaries. It is a piece of which Paul is particularly fond.

If Paul has an interest in something, he makes it his business to become an expert on it; this has led him to write many books, not only on ceramics, but also on railway journeys, northern France and Britain's canals. Other passions include early jazz, war memorials, printed ephemera, sculpture and gardening. Paul has two daughters, Polly and Zoe, and divides his time between London, the south coast and northern France.

Keith Baker miscellaneous

A hoarder of birds' eggs, comics, coins and stamps when he was a child, Keith is still a collector at heart, although he now looks out for American Indian beadwork and watercolours as a change from the objects he deals with as Head of Art Nouveau & Decorative Arts at Phillips. He began his working life first as a photographer and then as a computer specialist before joining Sotheby's European and Oriental Ceramics Department in 1972. He is a member of the Decorative Arts Society. His particular interest is in jewellery and accessories dating from 1860 up to the present day.

Rosemary Bandini pottery and porcelain

Rosemary joined the Insurance Department of Sotheby's after leaving Leicester University with a degree in Modern Languages. She then worked for two years in the Japanese Department and three years in Portrait Miniatures. After her two sons were born she joined her husband at Eskenazi Ltd, dealers in oriental works of art, developing an understanding of cataloguing collections and buying and selling. She is now an independent consultant working in association with the company, and is writing a book on netsuke. She enjoys learning languages and speaks Italian, French and some Japanese. Rosemary joined the *Roadshow* team in 1997.

Tony Banwell stamps

Tony grew up in Nottinghamshire and has been a collector of stamps since the age of six. He took a degree in Law at the University of Wales in Cardiff, and spent his vacations working in the retail stamp trade. In 1991, after 12 years at Christie's, Tony joined Sotheby's; he is now a Deputy Director, and senior expert in the Stamp Department, as well as an auctioneer. From 1979 to 1980 he was Director of Philatelic Services for Montserrat, with a brief to maximize the Caribbean island's revenue by improving the efficiency of the Post Office's philatelic division.

John Benjamin jewellery

John is International Director of Jewellery at Phillips, where he has worked since 1976. Just as he left school, his parents had occasion to buy his sister a piece of jewellery from Cameo Corner, the dealers in antique jewellery in Bloomsbury, central London. They encouraged John to write to them asking for a job, and he began his career there as an apprentice. He is a Fellow of the Gemmological Association, has a DGA (diploma in diamonds) and lectures in Britain and the United States. When time allows, he plays chess, which he adores, and listens to classical music.

David Battie pottery and porcelain *see page 25*

Hugh Bett books and manuscripts

In 1976, Hugh joined the London antiquarian booksellers Maggs Brothers Ltd as an assistant and is now a Director of the company. In addition to his general expertise in books he specializes in military and naval publications, and is currently the senior expert on travel and exploration literature. His work is also his hobby. Apart from enjoying spending time at his house in France, Hugh collects books on Ethiopia and hunts for ephemera connected with aviation.

Adam Bowett furniture

Adam read History at Oxford and York universities and became interested in furniture while working as a removals man after finishing his degree. He joined Phillips as a porter in the Furniture Department in 1987 and is now a furniture historian and research fellow at Brunel University; he first appeared on the *Roadshow* in 1997. He writes for a number of publications as well as finding the time to rebuild his house in the Wensleydale countryside and mend and ride motorcycles.

Roy Butler arms and armour

Roy began collecting at the age of eight, building a complete set of 50 Player's Military Head-dress cigarette cards. When the United Services Museum in Whitehall closed down in 1962, Roy bought six of the helmets from which the artist had drawn the illustrations for the cigarette cards. As an auctioneer he runs his own specialist auction house, Wallis and Wallis, and he owns one of the finest private collections of military head-dress in existence. Roy has been with the *Antiques Roadshow* since the first series.

Stephen Clarke silver

Stephen's career very much follows in the family tradition – his great-grandfather ran an antique shop in Guildford and acted as a freelance valuer, and his father still runs his own auction house, Clarke Gammon, in Guildford. Stephen started his career at Christie's South Kensington in 1978, becoming Head of the Silver Department at Christie's King Street in 1990 and a Director in 1992. He is now an independent fine art valuer in Surrey. As an antidote to antiques, Stephen plays tennis, cricket and golf.

John Bly furniture _____ *see page 28*
Penny Brittain miscellaneous _____ *see page 31*

Simon Bull clocks and watches _____ *see page 32*
Bunny Campione miscellaneous _____ *see page 36*

David Battie

David claims that his entire career has been a succession of accidents. He has never had the slightest ambition, he says, and even gives a lecture entitled 'My Unlikely Career'. After leaving school David trained as a graphic designer at Kingston School of Art, south-west London, and then worked for three years at *Reader's Digest*. 'I collected old books and decided I'd had enough of the rat race, so I got a job at Sotheby's in 1967 as a book porter. I thought of it as a way of dropping out.'

Despite this he's been dropping in ever since, visiting millions of living rooms around the country every Sunday as one of the longest-serving members of the *Roadshow* (he appeared on the first series). David moved rapidly from the Book Department to the Ceramics Department at Sotheby's during the early 1970s and married Sarah, a ceramics and glass expert. They have spent more than 20 years collecting together, their acumen occasionally enabling them to pounce on an overlooked bargain.

David's background in book design may be behind him, but books are still one of his major interests. As well as collecting a wide range of them, he is skilled at bookbinding. 'I converted my cellar into a bindery to store all the leather, gold leaf and tools – the fillets, gouges and rolls that you need to use in the process. When I bought the book on geometry (right) I knew that the original cloth binding was incredibly fragile, so I decided to make the hinged box you can see underneath it to contain the whole thing.'

David also puts his practical skills to good use in restoring antiques and other items, not only his own possessions, but also those of friends. Once again he retires to his workshop in the cellar, often taking on projects simply for the love of it and for the challenge. He is adept at reveneering, and admits that he likes 'repairing things that have gone wrong'.

▲ David's favourite object is this rare copy of *The First Six Books of the Elements of Euclid*. Published in 1847, it was an attempt to teach geometry using colour. 'The concept was unutterably silly,' says David, 'but it's a magical thing, an heroic failure, and I love it. I was knocked down by a motorcycle courier a few years ago and bought the book for $2,000 [£1,430] with the compensation money. It's a very fine example of Victorian colour printing.'

▲ David is holding a Lowestoft teapot of 1770 decorated with flowers. 'I've had this piece for 25 years. I bought it in an antique shop for a few pounds. The people who ran the shop didn't know what it was, and in those days neither did I! However, by this time I was working at Sotheby's as a "baby" cataloguer, so I knew it was early English porcelain, but I didn't recognize the factory.' On David's right is a mid-19th-century Florentine bookcase that was bought several years ago at auction. The figure painting on a gold-leaf ground harks back to the work of an earlier period, making this a typical Grand Tour piece. The bookcase holds part of David's collection of Victorian books, bought for either their decorative bindings or their illustrations. On top sits Sarah's magnificent ice pail, a Worcester blank, which was painted in 1834 and is highly unusual in being both signed and dated. Next to the ice pail stand a Regency Anglo-Indian ivory deer and a Satsuma vase.

James Collingridge silver

James started working at Debenham Storr (which became part of Christie's International in 1975) as an office boy at the age of 14 during the Second World War. After working during the day he attended evening classes in bookkeeping, which he then viewed as his future career. He went on to become a sales clerk, largely, he says, because everyone else was away at war, and in 1950, after National Service, returned to the company to work in silver and jewellery (which were then run as one department). He is now the Deputy Chairman of Christie's South Kensington, and is a specialist in silver and jewellery.

David Collins pictures and prints

David joined the Picture Department of the auction division of Knight, Frank and Rutley in 1965 as an office boy. In 1967 he became assistant to the picture valuer at Debenham Coe, taking over as Head of Department in 1971. He remained with the firm when it became Christie's South Kensington in 1975 and became a Director; in 1987 he became a member of the executive committee. An independent dealer and consultant since 1988, he appeared on the first series of the *Antiques Roadshow*. He regards the highlight of his career as running the sales of Tom Keating's (a famous faker and copyist) paintings at Christie's and Bonhams.

Margie Cooper miscellaneous

Margie is a general antiques dealer and consultant living in and working from Alderley Edge, Cheshire. Absorbed in this career for 20 years, she finds little time to spare for outside interests. She started her working life as a model for Wetherall and Jaeger, and began buying furniture and *objets d'art* for her own home as a hobby. Margie developed such a passion for antiques that she says she would have gone bankrupt had she not started selling as well as buying – she opened her business in 1978. Her great interest is English furniture, but she now deals mainly in silver and in Victorian and Edwardian jewellery.

Andrew Davis miscellaneous

Andrew trained as a lawyer and then worked as a teacher and an advertising copywriter before beginning to buy and sell clocks as a sideline. His interest in preserving objects grew until he began a career in antiques, repairing and transporting furniture and clocks around the country. He went on to run a stall in London's Portobello Road street market for two years and is now a general antiques dealer based in Kew, west London. His main interests are clocks, 19th-century ceramics and artefacts of 1700–1900, especially country furniture, and he is a member of the Regional Furniture Society.

Alastair Dickenson silver

Alastair is an independent dealer in the West End of London, specializing in antique silver. He started in the antiques business in 1971, after applying for a job at Phillips and being taken on as post boy. He then became a porter in the Silver Department and was promoted to cataloguer within months. He has also been a Director at both Asprey and Tessiers and lectures widely, particularly on fakes. A sport fanatic, Alastair was once a keen player of both rugby and cricket; he now pursues the gentler pastime of breeding border collies in the Surrey hills with his wife and exhibiting at Cruft's.

Clive Farahar books and manuscripts

A leading specialist in fine and rare books, Clive served his apprenticeship at one of London's most established antiquarian booksellers, Francis Edwards Ltd, becoming a partner in 1979. Now in private practice, he lectures at London University on the postgraduate course in Antiquarian Bookselling and also writes articles on the subject. At his home in the country he breeds rare poultry and collects African tribal artefacts. Clive also has a passion for the unspoilt Indian Ocean, particularly the islands of Mauritius and Réunion, and he hopes to visit Madagascar in the near future.

Josephine Fitzalan Howard pictures and prints

After reading History of Art at Bristol University, Josephine spent a year in Florence studying the same subject before joining the Old Master Paintings Department of Sotheby's, where she gained her auctioneer's licence. In 1990 she moved to the London picture dealers P & D Colnaghi, and she is now an independent fine art consultant as well as working part time for the international firm of Konrad Bernheimer Ltd. Josephine has three children and is Trustee of the children's charity Hemi-Help, which raises money for children with hemiplegia, a form of cerebral palsy. Half Danish, she enjoys collecting 18th-century Flora Danica porcelain.

Pat Frost textiles

Pat received a BA in English Literature, Life and Thought from Cambridge University and began working at Christie's South Kensington in 1986 as PA to the chairman. She moved on to the Textiles Department in 1988 as administrator and cataloguer, and introduced many new subject areas, such as Street Fashion and Needlework Tools. Pat now runs the Oriental and Islamic Costume and Textiles Department and joined the *Roadshow* in 1997. She speaks fluent French and German and collects stoles, particularly late-18th-century French and Macclesfield silk ones, as well as embroideries from the Greek islands.

John Bly

Where better to catch up with the man who claims to live with one foot in the 20th century and one in the 18th than at his shop in St James's in the West End of London? The premises are a shrine to Georgian elegance.

John Bly represents the third generation of a family of antique dealers. It was his grandfather who established the business in Tring, Hertfordshire, in 1891, and the tradition was carried on by John's father. John still keeps a showroom, offices and workshops at Tring, but he took the family business one step further when he opened his London shop in 1990. The premises are designed as a series of rooms, which have been filled with the objects for which he has most affection, mainly pieces from the 17th and 18th centuries.

Although perhaps best known as a furniture expert, John has also gained a great knowledge of silver, ceramics and objects of virtu (a term used to describe collector's items that show particular artistic virtuosity). He spent several years at Sotheby's at the start of his career, where he worked in various departments before leaving the auction house to concentrate on his family business.

John is also an accomplished jazz drummer, and considered turning professional at one stage. 'I have played the drums for more years than I care to remember, but, once I realized that I wasn't going to be the best jazz drummer in the world, I decided it should remain a passionate hobby. I'm still playing and still enjoying it, but I know I made the right decision.' His son James has inherited his musical talent and is a very good keyboard player. He and John frequently get together to play into the small hours.

John travels around Britain and overseas on buying trips, but manages to fit frequent lectures into his extremely busy schedule. He is, in addition, a Fellow of the Royal Society of Arts and a Liveryman of the Worshipful Company of Goldsmiths.

▲ John is sitting in one of a pair of English walnut armchairs, c.1675. To his left is an English satinwood and partridge-wood *bonheur du jour*, or lady's writing table, of about 1795, which has little silver handles and shows the influence of Sheraton. To his right is a magnificent Italian marble carving of two lions, c.1820, in the classical style. 'It's very much a Grand Tour thing and I love it,' says John. 'I also like old Sheffield plate, such as this little wine goblet of 1780.'

◀ 'Isn't this just the prettiest dumb waiter ever made?' says John of this English mahogany example of 1765. 'The dumb waiter is essentially a masculine piece of furniture, but this has such delicacy, and is perfectly proportioned. It was an incredible feat of engineering to create the fluted turning on the baluster, especially as all the work was done on a foot-operated lathe.'

Geoffrey Godden pottery and porcelain

Generally regarded as a leading authority on English ceramics, Geoffrey is the author of the classic *Encyclopaedia of British Pottery and Porcelain Marks* (1964). He is the third generation of his family to deal in antiques – his grandfather began the business in Worthing in 1900. On his last day at school, Geoffrey left at lunchtime and began working for his father at 2.15pm the same day. He has an honorary doctorate awarded by Keele University and is a visiting professor at the Southampton Institute; he joined the *Antiques Roadshow* in 1997. Geoffrey was a keen sea fisherman and is now a dedicated bowls player and umpire.

Bill·Harriman arms and armour

Bill attributes his interest in firearms to his grandfather, who owned a cinema and fired blanks from a gun at the appropriate moment during silent movies. Bill is now Head of Firearms for the British Association for Shooting and Conservation, which is based near Wrexham, North Wales. He is also an independent consultant specializing in all firearms, a Law Society expert witness and a member of the Academy of Experts, the leading body for expert witnesses. He trained initially as a chartered surveyor before completing Christie's Fine Art Course. Choral music and real ale are among his other interests.

Ian Harris jewellery

For many years Ian has run the family silver and jewellery business, N Bloom & Sons, in London's West End. He received a thorough training in English antique silver and old Sheffield plate. In the 1960s the firm diversified into antique jewellery, which is now Ian's major interest. He has published two books on silver and is a Freeman of the Worshipful Company of Goldsmiths and of the City of London. Known for his flamboyant octopus jewellery, Ian collects other octopus memorabilia, including bronzes and netsukes, and enjoys sailing his dinghy off the Sussex coast.

Natalie Harris jewellery

Natalie, who is married to Ian Harris, has been dealing in fine jewellery for 20 years, both independently and in association with N Bloom & Sons. She studied enamelling and silversmithing at London's Sir John Cass Goldsmiths' College and went on to learn the art of enamel restoration, specializing in Art Nouveau translucent and *plique à jour* enamelling. She is also a Fellow of the Gemmological Association and collects 19th-century textiles, especially beadwork. She has a fine collection of Indian beadwork and glass obelisks.

Jane Hay pottery and porcelain

Jane left her native Glasgow to take a degree in Modern History and Economics at Manchester University. She then did an MA in African Studies at the School of Oriental and African Studies in London and joined Christie's in April 1987. She worked in the Decorative Arts Department until 1995 and in the Ceramics Department until 1998, when she moved to Christie's St James's (joining the *Roadshow* in the same year). She is currently Business Manager in the Old Master Picture Department as well as being a Director of the company. Jane is a self-confessed crossword addict, plays the double bass and devours detective novels.

Rosamund Hinds-Howell miscellaneous

Rosamund has spent all of her working life in the art world, both in galleries and in public relations. She studied at Kingston Art School before joining Sotheby's, accumulating her knowledge of antiques while running the Valuations Counter, where she dealt with ceramics and glass as well as oriental objects and works of art. She also worked as senior press officer at Sotheby's, leaving in 1984. She spent six years at the Christopher Wood gallery and now works on a part-time basis for William Drummond, a long-established leading dealer in watercolours. Rosamund lives in London and is passionate about opera and gardening.

Philip Hook pictures and prints

Philip grew up visiting art galleries and museums, and drew and painted into adulthood, only giving up when he felt humbled by the masterpieces he came across in his working life. He read History of Art at Cambridge before joining Christie's. Philip became an independent dealer in 1987 and was a co-founder of the London-based St James's Art Group. He is now a Director of Sotheby's, and also a successful novelist; his latest book is *The Soldier in the Wheat Field*. An ardent supporter of Chelsea Football Club, he lives in a house that overlooks the ground. Philip appeared on the first series of the *Antiques Roadshow*.

John Hudson miscellaneous

John joined Christie's in 1965 behind the front counter and has worked with antiques ever since. Formerly a Director of Christie's South Kensington, where he was in charge of their Outside Valuations Department, he is now a regional representative for Sotheby's. He is a generalist, but is particularly interested in obscure medieval items and has written a dissertation on Herrengrund cups, the name given to small gilt copper vessels made by craftsmen in the area of the same name in the early 17th century. He also collects 18th-century white porcelain figures and art reference books.

◀ On the oak cricket table beside Penny sit two of her most treasured possessions, a Regency penwork writing slope and an Italian porcelain turkey group that was given to her by her mother. 'It was her favourite piece,' she recalls, 'but she gave it to me because she knew I loved it, so I treasure it all the more.'

▼ 'This bird-bath was the first present my husband ever gave me. I absolutely love it and so do the birds! It's modern, made by a craftsman called Chris Marvel, who lives and works in East Anglia. The material is some kind of resin, I think, but with a marble-like feel and texture. It sits on a chimney-pot in the garden and we're forever filling it up with fresh water, because the little bronzed birds attract all sorts of other birds, and they all splash about together.'

Penny Brittain

Penny had the good fortune to grow up with two wisely appointed godfathers. They were fervent collectors who fostered in her a love of antiques and fine things.

After leaving school she worked with an architect and interior designer, and then trained as a porcelain restorer. She married and had a family, and when her sons were old enough to go to school she took a one-year Christie's Fine Arts course before setting up the auction rooms for Cheffins Grain & Comins in Cambridge; it is now a major regional saleroom. 'I was there to watch the building going up,' recalls Penny, 'and I built the business up from scratch, doing the valuations, the cataloguing and the selling.'

The experience of helping to establish a business proved to be an invaluable one. Before long Penny was asked by the London auctioneers Phillips to set up its East Anglian headquarters. Eight years ago she started another business, this time founding her own company, called The Art and Antiques Service, which specializes in all aspects of buying, selling and valuing antiques.

'I think that my pioneering days are over now!' she laughs. 'I've got two young people joining me in my business, and after that I'll work with them as a consultant.' This will leave her more time to devote to the home she loves, a converted thatched stable in an idyllic corner of the English countryside.

Penny clearly realizes her good fortune in living in such a location and in so beautiful a house: 'It's a very unusual single-storey space. All of the rooms open onto the walled garden at the back, which is very much a part of the house. There is also a lovely Victorian greenhouse at the end of the garden that contains the most glorious vine.' Such is the attraction of the house, however, that space is often at a premium. 'My husband and I have five children between us,' says Penny, 'and they all drop in at various times. Unfortunately there are only two bedrooms, so the weekends can be hell! It's first come, first served for the only spare bed.'

Simon Bull

At the time of writing, Simon and his wife had not long completed the daunting task of restoring their house as it would have appeared around 1820, when it had its Regency face-lift. They undertook nearly all of the work themselves. 'There was a settlement on the site in 1600, and some bits of that are still here,' Simon explains, 'but what were two cottages were connected and faced up in 1720.'

Simon is known as a world authority on clocks and watches, but all things mechanical hold some fascination for him. He owns vintage cars and manages the Formula One racing car driven by Jackie Stewart in 1972, which now competes regularly in a European championship. At the age of 18 he was looking after the racing cars of a patron whose second passion happened to be clocks and watches; it was in this way that he came to develop the expertise for which he is known today.

In 1969 Simon joined Christie's, helping to set up their Clocks, Watches and Scientific Instruments Department. He left in 1976 in order to work as an independent dealer and consultant. Recently he became a consultant to Leroy, a French watchmaking company that has been in business since 1764 and was relaunched not long ago.

Simon is an enthusiastic collector of early timepieces, such as this French table clock (right), which probably dates from the late 15th century. 'Pieces like this were only made for the wealthiest of customers,' he says, showing an entirely understandable pride in his possession of this magnificent object. 'In paintings of the period you will often see a small clock or watch sitting on a table. It is really acting as a status symbol. Showing that you had the wealth to possess something like this was the point – its timekeeping ability hardly mattered. After all, no one in the 15th century was rushing to catch a train or an aeroplane.'

Simon is one of the longest-standing members of the *Roadshow* team, having been on the programme since the first series.

▲ This hexagonal gilt-brass French striking table clock, with a mechanism that has been constructed entirely of iron, was probably made before 1500. 'It is one of my favourite objects,' says Simon. 'It's exceptionally early for a portable spring-driven clock, and there are not many like it left.'

▲ Simon is pictured here sitting in a Gainsborough armchair with one of his dogs, Alfie. The vivid yellow silk covering was produced by a French textile company, and is based on silks made in the 18th century by the same firm in exactly the same bright colours and patterns. The walls are covered in a cotton made in the United States, printed with oriental scenes and given a satin finish. On the shelves is a collection of archaic Chinese objects, which includes some small jade items and scientific instruments. Their exact purpose is unknown, but they are thought to have been used for mathematical and astrological calculations. 'You could pick these up in markets and so forth 25 years ago for very little,' says Simon. On his left, hanging on the wooden frame between the rooms, is a simple French barometer painted with the emblems of the French Revolution.

Brand Inglis silver

Brand is an independent silver dealer in the West End of London. He was educated at Westminster School, where he spent free time exploring the treasures at the Victoria and Albert Museum and the interior of Westminster Abbey. He was commissioned into the Seaforth Highlanders, and on his return to civilian life joined Spink, the fine art dealers, before going into partnership with the celebrated dealer Thomas Lumley. He is a Liveryman of the Worshipful Company of Goldsmiths and a past president of the British Antique Dealers Association. He enjoys searching for late-17th-century and George II Rococo furniture for his collection.

Sally Kevill-Davis pottery and porcelain

Having worked for nine years as a porcelain specialist at Sotheby's, Sally is in the process of recataloguing the English porcelain in the Fitzwilliam Museum, Cambridge. She has also written and lectured on many aspects of ceramics. Married to a vicar, she has three children, and since becoming a mother she has researched the history of food and tableware, cooking and childcare. Sally's book *Yesterday's Children* explores the antiques and history of childcare. She bought her first antique, a leather-bound book of poetry, as a small child for three old pence, because she liked its binding rather than its contents.

Eric Knowles miscellaneous

Eric began his career in his native Burnley in the early 1970s, working for an antiques shipper, before joining Bonhams as a porter in the Ceramics Department in the mid-1970s. He became a Director of Bonhams in 1984 and is now responsible for the Decorative Arts Department and General Business Development. Eric lectures regularly, is the author of many books and a fellow of the Royal Society of Arts. He is well known for his appearances on programmes such as *Going, Going, Gone* and *Going for a Song*. He also presents Channel Five's *Great House Game*.

Deborah Lambert furniture

Deborah comes from an arts-based background: her father was a Literary and Arts Editor of the *Sunday Times*, and her mother trained as an actress. She became interested in the visual arts during her teens and studied English Literature and Art History at university. In 1978, after a period as Visual Arts Officer for the London Borough of Camden, she joined the newly formed Christie's Fine Arts Course as a tutor, specializing in furniture. In 1986 she became the Director of one of Christie's diploma courses for the study of fine and decorative arts.

Hilary Kay miscellaneous see page 39

Gordon Lang pottery and porcelain

Gordon Lang is a senior tutor for Sotheby's Works of Art courses and has written books on various aspects of Chinese, Export and Imperial porcelain, subjects for which he has gained an international reputation. He contributes articles to various magazines on the subject and is a consultant editor to *Miller's Antiques Price Guide*. Gordon is also an Honorary Keeper of the collection at Burghley House in Stamford, Lincolnshire, and a *Roadshow* expert since the third series. Reading, from modern American fiction to Italian and Chinese history, and cooking, particularly Italian and French cuisine, are hobbies.

Graham Lay miscellaneous

Graham joined the provincial auctioneers King and Chasemore in 1975 as reception porter, a time-honoured entry into the antiques business. He moved to London in 1978, when Sotheby's took over the firm, and later became the Head of the Auction Valuation Department for their Sussex saleroom. In 1988 he joined Bonhams and is now a Director; he is also the Managing Director of their auction rooms in the Channel Islands. He and his wife Alison are great animal lovers and at their Sussex home keep a menagerie of rescued animals, including horses, cats, dogs, chickens and parrots.

Victoria Leatham miscellaneous

Victoria is the Curator of the Burghley House, Lincolnshire, collection and is currently revising and cataloguing it; she also organizes regular exhibitions of its treasures in Great Britain and overseas. She is a consultant for Sotheby's, a lecturer, an author and a trustee of Stoneleigh Abbey and the Wellington Museum, and runs her own antique reproduction and mail-order business. Keen on interior design and the decoration of old houses, she has decorated the staterooms at Burghley and is about to tackle the open apartments at Stoneleigh Abbey. Passionate about dogs, she aims to run a rescue centre for spaniels if and when she retires.

Terence Lockett pottery and porcelain

Terence's first career was as a history teacher at a grammar school. He then spent 14 years training teachers before helping to set up the degree course in the History of Design at Manchester Metropolitan University. Terence is now a collector and President of the Northern Ceramic Society, and lectures to many antique collectors' societies in Britain and overseas, and is a Fellow of the Royal Society of Arts. He is also an author and has written books on Victorian tiles, Rockingham and Davenport. Fell walking is a great love and he has climbed every one of the 214 peaks in the Lake District described in Wainwright's ramblers' guides.

Frances Lynas pottery and porcelain

After reading English and History of Art at Glasgow University, Frances began her career in antiques by working for a London dealer before joining Phillips, where she worked for five years. She then worked for two years at Sotheby's, with particular responsibility for British ceramics. She is active in the French Porcelain Society and the English Ceramics Circle, and is a member of the vetting committee for the Olympia Art and Antiques Fair. Currently living in Madrid, she has spent the past 18 months acquiring fluency in Spanish and working as an independent consultant.

Rupert Maas pictures and prints

A fine art dealer, Rupert works from his gallery in the West End of London, which was started by his father, Jeremy, in 1960. The gallery specializes in Victorian art, and Rupert has organized a number of exhibitions there, including 'John Ruskin and his Circle', 'Pre-Raphaelites and Romantics', 'Victorian Paintings', 'British Illustrators' and 'Burne Jones'. He took a degree in Art History at Essex University and is a member of the executive committee of the Society of London Art Dealers. A keen sailor, he has completed an Atlantic crossing, and, while on dry land, enjoys carpentry and classical music.

Hugo Marsh toys and collectables

Hugo began collecting Hornby-Dublo trains and other railway artefacts as a teenager and never lost the bug. He worked first for Phillips, specializing in collectors' items, including toys, scientific instruments and photography. Hugo joined Christie's South Kensington as a toy specialist in 1989 and is now an Associate Director and Head of the Toy Department. He has written a number of articles on his subject and was the consultant for *Miller's Antiques Checklist: Toys & Games*. Victorian architecture and the restoration of ancient buildings are his great loves, and he used to collect obscure objects such as telegraph-pole insulators.

Elizabeth Merry books and manuscripts

Elizabeth's love of books began when she spent long periods confined to bed with a lung complaint as a child and read voraciously to pass the time. After gaining her degree, she learnt the book trade at Bernard Quaritch, the well-known London firm of antiquarian booksellers, before working for Christie's in Europe and London. She then spent ten years as an independent consultant before joining Phillips in 1990, where she is Head of the Book Department and an Associate Director. Her favourite areas include books on natural history and herbals, and she is a keen plantswoman and walker.

◄ Although Bunny would love to have a parrot, this is impossible at the moment, since she is constantly travelling around the world. Instead she contents herself with owning this magnificent 18th-century cast-iron birdcage – shown to her right – which she keeps in the conservatory at her home. 'I bought the cage ten years ago at the Olympia Antiques Fair,' she says. 'It's supposed to have come out of a Provençal monastery. The clock once worked, and the little feeders swivel round. It's sitting on a low table that I inherited from my mother, which is also 18th century and is supposed to have been used as a server for a whole spit-roasted suckling pig. I don't know whether that's strictly true, but it was always known as the "pig carrier" in my family!'

▼ Bunny bought this charming late-18th-century Italian miniature fitted chest at Olympia seven years ago. 'You might well pay a little more at Olympia,' she says, 'but where else would you find so many genuine and wonderful antiques under the same roof? I love this little chest and use it. Its surface is decorated in what is known as *arte povera*, or poor man's lacquer, a process by which prints are stuck onto the piece of furniture and are then simply painted and lacquered. The chest is 36cm (14in) by 41cm (16in) and is fitted with graduated drawers.'

Bunny Campione

Because Bunny Campione is best known by *Roadshow* viewers as an expert in the field of antique dolls and teddy bears, it comes as rather a surprise to learn that furniture – and particularly early English furniture – is actually her first love.

Bunny went to university in France and then spent a year working at the innovative Bear Lane Gallery in Oxford before joining Sotheby's in London in the 1970s. 'In those days,' she recalls, 'dolls and automata were included as part of the furniture sales, so I began learning about them at that time. Women furniture experts quite simply didn't exist then, so, although I was valuing and cataloguing furniture, I gravitated naturally towards the dolls, and in 1981 Sotheby's asked me to start a dedicated Doll Department.'

Bunny is now a consultant to the Valuation Department at Christie's South Kensington, and travels all over the world in the course of her work. 'I'm having such fun because I'm now handling all sorts of things, including furniture, and I never stop learning,' she says. In addition she runs her own antiques and fine art consultancy, finding individual objects for clients as well as selling a wide range of pieces. Her only regret is that her work leaves her insufficient time to spend at home or to pursue her many other interests. She enjoys skiing, plays a mean game of tennis and bridge, and is currently also learning golf – a process, she says, that is fraught with frustration!

It is well known that Bunny has an impressive collection of 70 soft rabbits, including ten important early Steiffs. Her love of rabbits took root at a very young age, and proved so enduring that it became the inspiration for the name by which she is always known. When she was a little girl, only just beginning to walk and talk, her parents gave her a dark-brown rabbit-fur coat with a hood that revealed a pair of rabbit's ears when it was pulled up over her head. From the very first day she put the coat on, she would only answer to the name of Bunny, and the name has stuck firmly ever since.

Bunny has now stopped buying rabbits and has turned her attention instead to collecting corkscrews, but furniture is still her favourite area. 'It's beautiful and practical and, if you buy carefully, a good investment which you can realize if you need to.'

Alan Midleton clocks and watches

Alan became Curator of Horology at the John Gershom Parkington Memorial Collection of Time Measurement Instruments in Bury St Edmunds in 1986. He remembers discovering in his school library, at the age of ten, a book on clocks that sparked his interest in the subject. He went on to take apart and put back together a clock belonging to his grandfather, but his career in horology did not begin until after short spells in the sugar industry in Argentina and banking in London. He then studied Technical Horology at Hackney Technical College and is now a Fellow and Vice-Chairman of the British Horological Institute.

Nicholas Mitchell miscellaneous

Nicholas has a very broad knowledge of antiques, having spent all his working life in the trade. For over 20 years he has been involved in almost every facet of antiques, from owning a shop to working as an auctioneer, and from restoring pieces to giving lectures to others on the subject. His areas of greatest knowledge and expertise include clocks – on which he has written articles for the specialist magazine *Antique Collector* – and 19th-century furniture. Nicholas lives near the River Thames in London and canoes on the river. He is also a keen cyclist, and holds a pilot's licence.

Hugo Morley-Fletcher pottery and porcelain

After reading Fine Arts at Trinity College, Cambridge, Hugo joined Christie's in 1963. He spent almost 28 years in their European Ceramics Department – where his posts included Head of European Ceramics and Glass, and Head of the Rome office – and became a Director of the company; Hugo is now a consultant to Christie's. He first appeared on *Going for a Song* in 1965 and was a frequent guest on *Collectors' World*; he joined the *Antiques Roadshow* for the first series. He has also appeared on *Mastermind*, choosing Italian Renaissance architecture as his specialist subject.

Barbara Morris miscellaneous

Barbara kept a museum in her bedroom from the age of six. The exhibits included birds' eggs, an 18th-century snuff spoon, stones from the Khyber Pass and shards of Roman pottery. She studied at the Slade School of Art before joining the Victoria and Albert Museum, and retired as Deputy Keeper of Ceramics and Glass in 1978. In 1979 she set up Sotheby's 19th and 20th Century Decorative Arts course and became principal of the short courses. She is a committee member of the Decorative Arts Society and first appeared on the *Roadshow* during the third series.

Geoffrey Munn jewellery *see page 42*

Peter Nahum pictures and prints

Peter began his career at Sotheby's in 1966. During his 17 years there he started the Victorian Painting Department and ran the British Painting Department. He was also Senior Director on the Chairman's committee and adviser on Victorian paintings to the British Rail pension fund. In 1984 he left Sotheby's to open his own gallery in St James's, specializing in paintings, drawings and sculpture from the 19th and 20th centuries. Peter also designs frames, writes and lectures, and first appeared on the *Antiques Roadshow* during the third series. He is a serious gardener and hopes to visit Japan to study the country's best gardens.

Michael Newman miscellaneous

Michael was born in Birmingham and moved to the West Country at the age of 11 to go to school. At 19 he became the youngest-ever qualified chartered auctioneer, winning the President's Award in the specialist antiques section. Since then Michael has worked all over Britain and Europe and now runs his own firm of fine art auctioneers and valuers in Plymouth. He is also an Associate of Bonhams. He lectures and broadcasts regularly on a range of subjects. An experienced generalist, he particularly loves English silver. He is a keen sailor and lives overlooking the River Yealm.

Christopher Payne furniture

Christopher belongs to the third generation of a family of furniture experts, his grandfather having opened a shop in 1901. He began his career at Sotheby's, where he stayed for 25 years, becoming a Director of the Furniture Department. Christopher is now a private fine art consultant advising clients internationally. He is the author of several books and General Editor of *Sotheby's Encyclopaedia of Furniture*, and is currently undertaking research projects into a variety of French furniture. When time allows, he skis, swims, plays tennis and rides his recently acquired Harley-Davidson motorcycle.

Sebastian Pearson pottery and porcelain

Sebastian first worked as a porcelain specialist and valuer for Sotheby's before moving to Bonhams, where he became a Director. He also worked as a dealer in Chinese works of art throughout the 1980s. He now runs a gallery in Cambridge, concentrating primarily on paintings and works of art. He regularly holds exhibitions showing the work of well-established living British artists while maintaining an interest in the oriental art market. Outside interests includes travelling, particularly in the Middle East and India, and classical music. Sebastian first appeared during the second series of the *Antiques Roadshow*.

Hilary Kay

Hilary Kay, a Senior Director of Sotheby's, has her grandfather to thank for her long and successful career as a specialist and auctioneer. It was his microscope (below) that sparked her early interest in things mechanical and scientific.

'I was the only granddaughter amongst several grandsons and was always treated as if I were one of the boys. We had hours of fun examining pond life under the microscope, but I was always fascinated not so much by what I could see through the lenses, but by the way the microscope was constructed. I wanted to know exactly how it worked, how the rack and pinions engaged with one another and how all the accessories functioned. I also loved it as an object, with its gleaming brass, and was impressed by the obvious skill involved in making it.'

Although as a teenager Hilary knew that she wanted a career in the antiques business, she did not realize how much opportunity there would be to develop not only her knowledge of mechanical objects, but also her ability to lead a team of people. 'I had a place at university, but took a year out after leaving school to work in London. Towards the end of that year I got a job at Sotheby's and, thinking that the opportunity might not arise again, decided to postpone university.'

She joined Sotheby's newly formed Collectors' Department in 1977, at a time when objects such as microscopes, typewriters, gramophones, cameras and magic lanterns were beginning to fetch reasonable amounts at auction. Toys, dolls and games were also beginning to be taken seriously by antique dealers, and Hilary afforded them the same enthusiasm she did every other category of collectable in those early days. By the age of 20, Hilary was head of the Department. David Battie, in charge of Sotheby's branch in Belgravia, was her boss for the first three years.

Like so many experts on the *Roadshow* (she joined during the third series), Hilary has a broad approach to antiques. Apart from the areas dearest to her heart, she

▲ Hilary with one of her favourite possessions, a carved wooden Noah's Ark made during the 1840s in the Erzgebirge region of eastern Germany. 'What makes it exceptional,' she says, 'is that it includes around 350 animals, ranging from elephants down to ladybirds with everything in between. I bought it a few years ago at auction and it gives me enormous pleasure.'

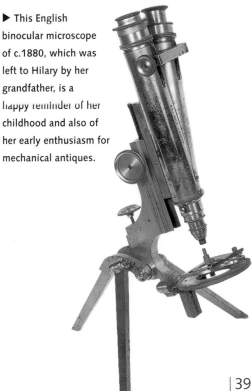

▶ This English binocular microscope of c.1880, which was left to Hilary by her grandfather, is a happy reminder of her childhood and also of her early enthusiasm for mechanical antiques.

enjoys and lives with pieces of English folk art and treen. These range from carved biscuit moulds and painted Punch and Judy heads that date from the middle of the 19th century to a variety of samplers and naïve paintings. Another of Hilary's passions is driving, and when she recently moved from London to live in the country her tired but beloved old Mercedes made the move with her.

Ian Pickford silver

Ian bought a small French character jug when he was four, the first of many treasures accumulated during his childhood – he still has his collection of bus tickets. On leaving school he was destined to read Physics at university but followed his instincts and his growing interest in silver by joining Shrubsoles, a leading retailer of antique silver near the British Museum. Six years later he became a lecturer in silver for the universities of London and Surrey, for NADFAS (National Association of Decorative and Fine Art Societies) and for the National Trust. Ian has written many books and is editor of *Jackson's Silver and Gold Marks*.

Mark Poltimore pictures and prints

Mark worked with his godfather in a small gallery before joining Christie's in 1978 to deal with their Old Master, English and 19th-century pictures and watercolours. In 1988 he became Head of the Victorian and Continental Pictures Department, and he was made a director of the company in the same year. Mark instigated the first sales of Symbolist, Scandinavian and 19th-century Spanish pictures, and he was behind Christie's first sale of Greek pictures, which was held in Athens. A keen reader and film-goer, Mark is also a devotee of pop music and still finds time to play the drums in a band.

Justin Pressland toys and collectables

An independent dealer in modern and antique toys, Justin had a 1970s childhood that exerted a great influence on his tastes. He began dealing in toys from this period, including James Bond, Corgi, Dinky, Action Man, Scalextric and other items related to popular culture, including music. Innumerable visits to fairs, often in the USA, have expanded his expertise. A self-confessed product of the TV age, he regularly appears on television and writes for specialist magazines on modern collectables. He also collects vinyl records, hi-fis and digital watches, and is the proud owner of three classic cars.

Richard Price clocks and watches

Richard joined Bonham's in London in 1975 and started its Clock Department. As manager and consultant he was responsible for all valuations and sales for 17 years. After a short spell trading in Portobello Road and Grays Antique Market he now exhibits at major London antiques fairs, notably the three fine art fairs held annually at Olympia. He is also actively involved in aviation, which allows him to travel extensively and find unusual and interesting clocks throughout Europe. He lectures regularly to police forces, helping them to understand clocks and also to recover stolen pieces.

Orlando Rock furniture

Orlando claims that his interest in the decorative arts was ignited by being dragged round museums and art galleries as a child by his parents. He joined Christie's after completing a degree in History at Bristol University; he is now a director of the company and regularly lectures for its Education Department. Orlando specializes in English and European furniture, tapestries and ormolu mounted objects of 1550–1840. He is particularly interested in the English country house and architecture of the late 17th and the 18th century, and has made a study of the history of patronage and collecting.

Barley Roscoe miscellaneous

The great-great niece of the celebrated Cotswold School furniture designer Ernest Gimson, Barley grew up enjoying the arts, going to silversmithing classes and learning textile printing from the age of 13. After university at Bristol she studied woven and printed textiles at the Surrey Institute of Art and Design at Farnham, and then established the craft collection and archive at the Holburne Museum and Crafts Study Centre in Bath, where she is now Director. She is also an Associate of the Museums Association and a Fellow of the Royal Society of Arts, and was awarded an MBE in 1993 in recognition of her work at the Holburne Museum.

James Rylands miscellaneous

James joined Sotheby's after gaining a degree in History of Art at Reading University and spent two years working in Torquay for what was then Sotheby Bearnes. He then moved to Sotheby's Sussex saleroom, where he was instrumental in starting up the sales of garden statuary in 1986. A Director of the company, he now divides his time between London and Sussex, appears regularly on television and writes for magazines. He collects antique lavatories and is a keen scuba diver and treasure hunter on wrecks off the coast of Bermuda.

John Sandon pottery and porcelain

John collected fossils as a boy and grew up with a love of geology and palaeontology. He is a specialist in English and Continental pottery, porcelain and glass at Phillips in London and the Director of their Ceramics and Glass Department. He has been with the company since leaving school. John's subject is as much a hobby as a profession; he also lectures widely and has written a number of books on Worcester porcelain. His latest book, *Starting to Collect Antique Glass*, is published by Antiques Collectors' Club. John is, of course, the son of Henry Sandon.

Henry Sandon pottery and porcelain see page 45

◀ Geoffrey's border terrier, Rosie, lies close by his side. Behind him is a blue chalk portrait of the Countess of Plymouth by Sir Edward Poynter, who was the brother-in-law of Edward Burne-Jones. 'I'm passionately interested in paintings,' Geoffrey says. 'They're beyond the reach of most of us, but you can still buy 19th-century drawings like this for a reasonable price.'

▼ Geoffrey loves 19th-century objects, especially Gothic Revival pieces. This pair of open-petalled brass and copper flowers, which he calls 'Triffids', was bought at Christie's five years ago. 'They're quite big,' Geoffrey says, 'about 7in [18cm] high with 6½in [16.5cm] diameter bowls. When the light falls into them it bounces out again, creating a wonderful effect.' The flowers are the work of W A S Benson, a leading Arts and Crafts metalworker who made lots of props for Pre-Raphaelite paintings, including the crown for Burne-Jones's famous *King Cophetua and the Beggar Maid*.

Geoffrey Munn

Geoffrey's keen wit and self-effacing manner make him one of the most popular members of the *Roadshow* team. After leaving school he joined Wartski, the leading firm of West End jewellers, where he worked as a junior. These days he is the company's Managing Director, but claims that he still sometimes makes the tea and vacuums the carpets!

After a long day spent peering at gems and taking care of customers and collectors, Geoffrey makes a beeline for home. He lives in a comfortable Victorian house with a large garden, which he shares with his wife Caroline and their two young sons. The Munn household also comprises two dogs, a parrot and an impressive collection of 14 bonsai trees.

The bonsais stay outside, well out of the reach of Keiko, the Munns' parrot. 'They're not that difficult to maintain, provided that you keep them outside,' Geoffrey claims. 'Apart from watering them occasionally, I probably only spend two days a year working on them.' He is proud of the fact that every one of the bonsais has been grown from saplings taken from his garden, with the exception of a maple that his wife gave him as a wedding present. He is currently attempting to strike mistletoe, a tricky task that can only be undertaken in early spring. 'I got the seeds from Petworth House,' he explains, 'then I cut into the bark of the apple tree and put them in, and now all I can do is wait patiently.'

Every week without fail Geoffrey visits his local auction rooms. 'You often have to spend a long time sifting through piles of rubbish,' he says, 'but you need to stay on your guard, because something can suddenly jump out at you.' He has certainly benefited from his perseverance and keen eye. 'We bought all the curtains in the house second-hand,' he says with some satisfaction. 'People get rid of them when they redecorate and you get the most wonderful fabric at a fraction of the cost of having new ones made.'

Stephen Somerville pictures and prints

After studying music and musical instrument making, Stephen joined Sotheby's Print Department in London and in 1965 became Head of the Print Department in New York. In 1967 he joined P & D Colnaghi to run the Department dealing with English painting, watercolours, prints and drawings. Since 1987 he has run his own gallery in the West End of London. He is Chairman of Friends of Prints and Drawings at the British Museum. Stephen plays tennis three or four times a week and dances (anything from Scottish country to salsa) at least once a week. He also plays the viola da gamba and enjoys English consort music of 1580–1660.

Chris Spencer pottery and porcelain

Chris nursed ambitions to be an actor but became a teacher instead. Two years ago he retired as a headmaster to work full time as an independent antiques dealer and valuer. He has been fascinated by ceramics since the early 1970s, when his father, who ran an antiques shop, gave him a bowl carrying a Worcester crescent mark to research. The piece was a Lowestoft copy, which led to Chris becoming an authority on Lowestoft porcelain. He is a member of the English Ceramic Circle and lectures and writes extensively on early English porcelains. His other major interest is in English paintings, particularly those of the Newlyn School.

Clive Stewart-Lockhart pictures and prints

At the age of 15, Clive saw an advertisement for a sale of modern paintings at Sotheby's, sent for the catalogue and determined from that moment to pursue a career in antiques. He joined Sotheby's on leaving school, and worked in their Ceramics Department for five years, interrupted by short periods at Bonhams and the porcelain dealers Bluett & Sons. Clive joined the auctioneers Dreweatt Neate in 1982 and is now Head of their Fine Art Department. His specialities include oriental ceramics, as well as works of art and pictures.

Philip Taubenheim miscellaneous

Philip's parents ran an antiquarian bookshop in the Oxfordshire town of Burford, so he gained much early experience of salerooms. On leaving school he worked for a firm of auctioneers in Cirencester and in 1982 joined the Fine Art Department of auctioneers Sandoe's, in Wotton-under-Edge, Gloucestershire. Three years ago he bought the company, which now trades as Wotton Auction Rooms. He is still interested in books and also collects treen, but currently devotes every moment to running his business.

Kerry Taylor miscellaneous

Kerry joined Sotheby's in Chester in 1979 as a junior receptionist. She went on to become a junior cataloguer in the Silver Department and started up their Collectors' Department in 1980. She was made Departmental Director and an auctioneer before moving to join the Collectors' Department in London in 1985. Since then she has organized exhibitions and the sale of many important collections, including the Castle Howard Diaghilev Ballet collection and the Chrysler Museum collection of *haute couture*. Kerry is now Head of the Costumes, Textiles, Toys and Dolls Department and a Deputy Director of Sotheby's.

Paul Viney miscellaneous

Paul began his career at the Ashmolean Museum in Oxford after two years backpacking in Australia followed by a course in Fine Arts at the Victoria and Albert Museum. He then worked for the National Trust at Waddesdon Manor, the former Rothschild house near Aylesbury, Buckinghamshire, before joining Phillips, where he was Vice President in New York for three years and European Director from 1986 to 1992. Paul is now Managing Director of Woolley & Wallis, the Salisbury auctioneers. He is well known for his annual Children in Need auctions, and lectures extensively on furniture, ceramics and pictures.

Peter Waldron silver

Peter is a Senior Director of Sotheby's and is responsible for silver, objects of virtu and portrait miniatures in Britain and Europe. He joined the firm as a junior administrator in 1966, but within two years was promoted to cataloguer in the Silver Department; he joined the *Roadshow* team during the second series. Peter is a Liveryman of the Worshipful Company of Goldsmiths and a Freeman of the City of London. He is fascinated by heraldry and researches armorials and family histories, and is a fan of cricket, tennis and horse racing.

Tim Wonnacott miscellaneous

Tim's father and grandfather were auctioneers in north Devon, and he has followed in the family tradition. He joined Sotheby's in 1978 and is now a full board director, working from their Chester office. Tim is a Fellow of the Royal Institute of Chartered Surveyors and an Associate of the Society of Valuers and Auctioneers. His specialist subjects include furniture, clocks and works of art, knowledge that he applies in pursuing his interest in interior decoration. He is a regular presenter on *The Antiques Show* and has appeared on *The Antiques Inspectors* and *Going Going Gone*.

Lars Tharp pottery and porcelain see page 46

Henry Sandon

When bombs began to fall on the capital during the Second World War, Henry Sandon, a Londoner born and bred, was evacuated to Buckinghamshire. While other children clutched their teddy bears for comfort, Henry packed his Donald Duck porcelain teapot. His instinct foretold a future as one of our best-loved ceramics experts.

There were, however, other ambitions to fulfil. Henry trained at London's Guildhall School and had a successful career as a singer and as a music teacher at Worcester Grammar School, and a lay clerk in the cathedral choir.

Archaeology was another of Henry's passions, and while he was excavating his garden in Worcester he uncovered several Roman pots. 'It was the most exciting thing, to find those pieces in my garden. I began to study and research ceramics of all kinds, which led me to the Royal Worcester factory.' Henry acquired such expertise that in 1966 he became Curator of the Dyson Perrins Museum at the factory, a position he held until 1982. He joined the *Roadshow*, meanwhile, during the second series.

'The age of a piece doesn't worry me, or its condition, but it must speak to me, tell me it wants to be found,' says Henry. 'Working at Royal Worcester, I met many of the artists and craftsmen, and now when I look at an object I'm able to say, "I remember him painting that plate or modelling that vase or figure." It gives me a tremendous thrill because it brings pieces alive if you imagine who made them and the people who used them.'

Henry's undying enthusiasm for pots still has him scouring shops and markets, and even beachcombing – every shelf and corner of his house is filled with his treasures. He is committed to keeping up the tradition of hand-made ceramics, and is a director of the Brontë Company in Malvern, a new porcelain factory set up by two old friends. A Henry Sandon candle extinguisher and a character jug have already been produced.

▶ One of Henry's great treasures, this plate is part of a unique dinner service made by Royal Worcester in 1926 for Kellogg of breakfast-cereal fame and shipped to him in the United States. The centre of the plate was decorated by Harry Stinton, whom Henry Sandon knew well. Stinton specialized in these Highland scenes, which are based on the paintings of Sir Joseph Farquharson. The service was sold after Kellogg's death and, when the buyer wanted to sell on, Henry arranged for it to be brought back to Britain. The new owner invited Henry and his wife Barbara to choose one of the dinner plates. Barbara made the final choice, and later, on a trip to Scotland, the Sandons were taken to the exact spot on the Finzean estate where Farquharson painted this scene.

▼ On the table in front of Henry sits the Donald Duck teapot, made by Wade in the 1930s, that he took with him when he was evacuated from London as a boy during the Blitz. Next to it is an Aesthetic teapot made by Royal Worcester in 1886. Among the pieces on the shelves behind Henry is a reproduction Ozzy the Owl drinking cup made for him by a potter in Wales.

Lars Tharp

Lars has a Danish mother and, until the age of six, lived in Copenhagen with his parents. His grandfather was a leading expert on the Danish Bronze Age and Keeper at the National Museum. It was through him that Lars became interested in archaeology. After leaving school he studied the subject at Cambridge University, graduating in 1976. Lars has always been a keen amateur cellist, however, and claims that he spent more time playing in concerts as a member of the university music society than going to tutorials. Like many students, he found that the prospects of employment related directly to his degree were limited.

'I specialized in the Stone Age and soon realized there weren't many jobs going for Stone Age archaeologists,' he says. 'However, I had always been interested in Chinese works of art, partly because the Master of my college was Joseph Needham, who was at the time the greatest-living Western expert on Chinese culture. I caught the bug and decided to learn more.'

The best way forward, Lars realized, was to join one of the major auction houses: 'I was taken on at Sotheby's as a junior cataloguer and moved to the Valuation Department after two years, specializing in Chinese ceramics.' He ran the Ceramics and Oriental Works of Art Department at Sotheby's Sussex saleroom and then spent time in the Musical Instruments Department, forging links between the department and professional musicians, before leaving Sotheby's to become an independent consultant.

Home is shared with his wife Gillian, his daughters Helena, eleven, and Georgina, five, and the family's two dogs – Fanny the stately golden retriever and Basil the black labrador, whose boisterous antics have played havoc with the polished wooden floor in the drawing room. The family live in a cottage with wonderful views across open, rolling countryside. Lars and his wife love opera and try to make several trips to Glyndebourne during the year.

▲ The work of William Hogarth is one of Lars's abiding passions – his book *Hogarth's China* describes the ceramics depicted in Hogarth's paintings and vice versa. The engraving on the wall behind him is the second in a series of six taken from Hogarth's *The Harlot's Progress*. In this scene, Moll Hackabout trips over a tea table, sending the precious Chinese porcelain crashing to the floor. On Lars's mantelpiece is a Staffordshire equestrian figure of c.1860; it was a farewell gift from the staff at Sotheby's Ceramics Department, who took the headless figure, attached a photograph of Lars and inscribed on the base: 'A Pride Goeth Before the Fall'. To the left of the Staffordshire figure are a black glazed jug and beer mug, a late-17th-century Chinese vase and a magnificent English delftware plate, c.1760, which was probably made in Bristol.

▼ While filming the American version of *The Great Antiques Hunt*, Lars found this wonderful Chinese *famille rose* porcelain wall vase, c.1820, in the form of a hand clutching a peach. The owner wanted $35 (£25) but knocked it down to $25 (£18) because she liked Lars's English accent. 'It's about 6in [15cm] long, worth £200–300, and I hang it on the wall and keep my pens in it,' he says.

Christopher Wood pictures and prints

A specialist in Victorian art, Christopher is the author of *The Dictionary of Victorian Painters*, the standard work of reference on the subject, in addition to many other books on painting. He joined Christie's in 1963, becoming Director of its 19th-Century Paintings Department. Since 1977 he has run his own business in London's West End and currently works privately, specializing in Pre-Raphaelite and Victorian art, and Gothic Revival and Arts and Crafts furniture. He has a Gothic Revival house that reflects his passion for the architecture of the period. His other interests include gardening and jazz.

Henry Wyndham pictures and prints

Before his appointment as Chairman of Sotheby's in 1994, Henry was an independent dealer, picture consultant and member of the London-based St James's Art Group. He was also formerly head of departments at Christie's in London and New York. His interests range from Old Masters to sporting pictures and work by young contemporary artists, including studio pottery. He is a member of the Goldsmiths' Livery Company, a Committee Member of the MCC and Chairman of the Arts and Library Committee of the MCC. Cricket, as evidenced by some of the above appointments, is his abiding passion.

Experts on reception

A number of experts fulfil the vital and demanding role of receiving customers at reception and directing them to the right area. Important objects are often identified at this stage.

Sonia Archdale

Sophie Farahar

Natalie Harris

Rosamund Hinds-Howell

Barley Roscoe

Deborah Scott

Philip Taubenheim

Sally Watson-West

Christine Yirrell

Alec Yirrell miscellaneous

Alec began his career as a teacher of physical education before becoming a lecturer in Professional Studies at a college of education. His interest in and knowledge of antiques burgeoned when he and his wife restored and furnished their first cottage in Derbyshire. In 1980 he took early retirement from teaching and became a general antiques dealer in Bath. His main interest is in collectables, small silver, objects of virtu and toys. Alec has been involved with the *Roadshow* since the second series, and has been front-of-house manager for 16 years.

Making the programme

◀ An expert and a customer stand by for the signal to begin their conversation as the main camera unit lines up to record a fine piece of furniture.

Ensuring that every member of the team and every piece of equipment arrives safely at every *Roadshow* venue is a daunting task. All of the different locations chosen for each series must be thoroughly researched in advance. By the time the public starts arriving on the day itself, every aspect of a site has been carefully considered and every potential technical problem anticipated and eliminated. Behind the scenes an experienced production team is on hand to deal with all aspects of the making of the programme, from its earliest planning stages, through the process of filming and editing, right up until the final tape is delivered to BBC headquarters in London and the programme is transmitted.

Planning the Roadshows

The filming of a series of the *Antiques Roadshow* takes place between April and November. Apart from a break during August, when many people are away on holiday, each week for those eight months of the year there is usually a show taking place somewhere in the country. While making sure that each event runs smoothly (and the *Antiques Roadshow* is the largest public gathering staged by the BBC), the production team are also planning the next series, editing the current one and running the office in Bristol.

Executive producer Christopher Lewis, producer Michèle Burgess, production manager Liz Nicol and press officer Nikki Jones go on every *Roadshow*. The teams of directors, production assistants and production secretaries rotate so that the office is never empty. Because everything must continue to run smoothly, there is never a day off to recover from the gruelling couple of days a week on the road. Everyone usually travels home to Bristol on Thursday evening when the day's event is over (unless the location is particularly far away) and works a full day on Friday.

During the first three months of the year the groundwork of finding suitable venues for the *Roadshow* takes place. It is essential that as many areas of the country as is feasible are covered in each series. To this end the database is consulted for past locations, and the trusty wall map, about as low-tech and hands-on as you can get, pored over. The team's mission is to get as many people as possible, within a radius of about 25 miles of the chosen place, to bring their heirlooms to the *Roadshow*.

Suggestions for venues are often sent in to the *Roadshow* by members of the public. The experts also have a hand in the process: often they contact the team to say they have given a lecture or carried out a valuation day at a particular place that seems to fit the bill. Over the last few years stately homes and castles have become dazzling arenas for *Roadshows* filmed in the open air, and in many cases the owners or managers of these historic sites made personal contact with the production office.

Each director and producer is allocated an area of the country. Every suggested location is researched, and if it sounds

suitable it is visited to assess size, ease of access, parking facilities and the number of visitors it might attract. Designer John Bone and engineering manager John Neal – inevitably 'the two Johns' – then make an initial technical reconnaissance; if the place passes muster on all counts it joins the list, and work begins to transform it into another attractive venue.

Once the list of locations is complete it is distributed to everyone involved, including the all-important experts, who tick the dates when they are available and return the list to Bristol within two weeks. The next stage is to book hotels, make travel arrangements for the experts and the team, notify the local press and radio, and distribute posters.

Six weeks before each *Roadshow*, with every detail attended to, a full production meeting takes place to anticipate and sort out any last-minute hitches. The *Roadshow* may have its own momentum, but this does not mean that anything is left to chance. By the time that all the equipment, members of staff and experts are in place on site, there will have been many weeks of careful planning.

▲ ▶ Broadcasting House in Bristol, the nerve centre of the *Antiques Roadshow*, is where each series is planned and later prepared for transmission.

▲ Executive producer Christopher Lewis and press officer Nikki Jones discuss publicity for the next series.

◄ Christopher Lewis gathers the team around him to bring them up to date on progress at venues around the country. He aims to hold one major meeting a month at which everyone must be present.

▲ The *Roadshow* is coming! A central feature of the programme's office is the wall map, dotted with pins marking the locations for each series.

◄ Left, back, producer Michèle Burgess; front, director Pete Smith; right, back, director Steve Potter; front, director Amanda Fidler.

► Director Karen Smallwood (left) and production manager Liz Nicol discuss arrangements for taking the show on the road. Catering for the needs of up to a hundred people every week for eight months requires meticulous organization.

Setting up at the location

In the grey, early gloom of Monday morning the first of the lorries from the BBC rumbles up to the location. A large, bare and deathly quiet space greets the men who deliver the scaffolding. They spend the day building the towers and arranging the network of poles across the roof space that allows the following team to do their job.

On Tuesday morning the lighting crew arrives to begin the long task of rigging the dozens of heavy five-kilowatt tungsten lamps used to light the event. It takes the electricians, or 'sparks', almost 12 hours to hoist the lamps on pulleys to the men at the top of the scaffolding towers who fix them in position. On the day of the show there is a specific lighting control for each camera position, and a console allows the entire array to be driven from the on-site production room.

By the afternoon, with only 24 hours left to prepare the venue, both the scanner (the mobile control room) and the lorry containing the set have arrived and parked. For a time the sparks work alongside the television operatives, or, more familiarly, 'TVOs' (the people who are responsible for arranging the scenery), and the space is filled with the noise of different groups with only one objective – to complete the mammoth task of transforming the venue within the deadline.

Inside the lorry, with its smart blue and white livery, the TVOs pin up and study the layout of the set that will guide them as they unload the scenery. Between 65 and 70 screens, or 'flats' as they are known, must be erected around the edges of the space and drapes hung to create the 'room' in which the show is recorded. The chairs are the only items to arrive in one piece – the tables, reception area and souvenir shop arrive in parts that must be slotted together.

With the lighting almost in place, and the set taking shape, the two Johns arrive in one vehicle. The entire layout of each *Roadshow* is the responsibility of designer John Bone, while engineering manager John Neal masterminds every technical aspect of the operation, including lighting and sound.

These two plan each location well in advance. Whereas some members of the team will see the venue for the first time when they arrive to set up, John and John may have made as many as three previous visits, along with Christopher Lewis, the executive producer. By working closely together in the planning stages the two of them avoid the practical and technical problems that could ruin the show. Out of 40 possible venues last year, only 30 met their rigorous criteria.

The enormous task of preparing the venue continues until, by Wednesday afternoon, the transformation is complete. Christopher Lewis gathers his production team about him to finalize last-minute details, and the front-of-house manager, Alec Yirrell, briefs the local helpers who, in various ways, will help the event to run smoothly. By early evening a tired but happy team retire for the night, with the scene set for another *Roadshow*.

▲ It's early Tuesday morning, and the lighting equipment is swiftly unloaded from the lorry before the crew begin rigging the dozens of heavy five-kilowatt tungsten lamps needed to light the show. The large, trunk-like pieces of apparatus are dimmer racks, each containing 36 dimmers. Inset: one of the 'six lights' is ready to be hauled into position.

▲ During rehearsal, John Neal stands at the temporary desk he sets up on Tuesday afternoon to pre-programme the lighting computer. On the day of the broadcast the various effects and treatments are in place.

▲ Charge-hand Peter Cartwright studies the plan of the hall. The position of each light has been carefully thought out by John Neal, who collaborates with John Bone to prevent any practical or technical problems from marring the day.

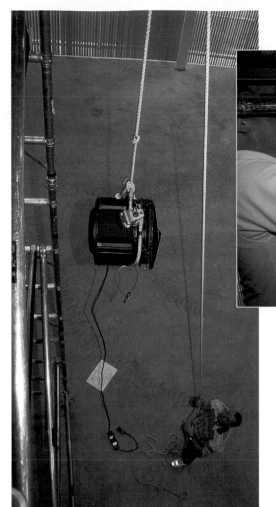

▲ Great care is needed when clamping the lights to the network of scaffolding that forms a canopy far above the main hall. It also helps to have a head for heights.

◄ The team begin to attach each lamp to a strong pulley so that it can be hoisted to the top of the scaffolding tower. It can take up to 12 hours to complete the job.

▲ The distribution unit relays power from the mains (or, when necessary, the generator) to the dimmers and back again to each individual light.

► The 'TVOs' park close to the hall and begin to unload the set, including the 70 or so 'flats' (plywood panels framed by lightweight aluminium) that must then be clipped together. Introduced in 1993, these screens replaced the wooden frames with braces that needed two men to lift them.

► Rob Looker rolls one of the tabletops down the ramp. Nearly every component of the set, including the reception area and the souvenir shop, breaks down for transportation. With skilful packing it stows neatly inside the lorry.

▲ Cameras stand forlornly to one side of the set. By Wednesday afternoon they will be manned and ready for the rehearsal that takes place at approximately 5pm. Every position that the cameras will occupy during the day of the shoot is tested to ensure that no fire exits or other unsightly features of the venue appear in shot.

▲ Designer John Bone finds a corner where he can work on his indispensable laptop computer, which he uses to design the set and layout of every venue. With everything in readiness here – apart from dressing the set with the furniture when it arrives on Wednesday afternoon – he uses a few quiet moments to develop ideas for future shows.

▲ The lights are in place, the scenery is set, the furniture has arrived (see pages 58–61), and a hectic Wednesday is finally drawing to a close. All that remains is to sort out any last-minute problems before the day of the Roadshow dawns.

▲ The finishing touches are, of course, very important. At every location, local helpers produce lavish flower arrangements that set off the furniture and paintings and give an extra lift to the set.

▲ Among the secrets of the *Roadshow* are meticulous planning and the pooling of the range of skills found in the teams of 'TVOs' and riggers. Back row, left to right: Barry Humphries, Kevin Parker, Clive Treacher, Stan Hamblen and Trevor Poole. Sitting, left to right: John Wood, John Sweet, Rob Looker, Glenn Ivers and Andy Bishop.

▲ At every venue Alec Yirrell (far right), the front-of-house manager, directs the team of local helpers – National Trust volunteers, girl guides, boy scouts, teachers and pupils, among others – who guide the public to the right areas, serve refreshments and otherwise contribute to the success of the day.

▶ Executive producer Christopher Lewis gathers his team about him, including directors, producers and the recording manager, for a final meeting late on Wednesday. They discuss the furniture round, the characteristics of the location and the strategy for the next day.

Hugh Scully's introduction

First thing on Wednesday morning the 'portable single-camera unit', or 'PSC', consisting of the cameraman, his assistant and the sound recordist, sets off with one of the directors (four work in rotation). They will spend the day filming the views of the area surrounding the venue that give each *Roadshow* its unique character.

Well in advance of the day of the shoot the director will have visited the locality to research its history, landmarks and any sites of national importance. The house of a famous politician or writer, an important local industry or an area of outstanding beauty – all can be used to add bring out the individuality of a venue.

The research notes are forwarded to Hugh Scully, who then discusses his ideas for the introduction with the director by telephone before arriving to join the team. 'Wednesday is my busiest day,' he says. 'On the day of the *Roadshow* I like to stay in the background. I think the essence of the event is the communication that takes place between the customers and the experts, but the day before we work as a team to get across the character and the history of a place and a sense of the people who live there.'

Hugh's introduction at the beginning of the programme, and his farewell at the end, are completely unscripted. He waits until he arrives at a location, gets a feeling for it and then walks away from the rest of the crew for a few minutes. As he paces about, he composes the monologue in his head, waits for the director's countdown and then does his 'piece to camera', or 'PTC', completely unrehearsed.

The crew spend time on Wednesday shooting 'general views' ('GVs'). During the *Roadshow* on Thursday, Hugh writes a number of voice-overs that are recorded outside the hall to make certain that the acoustics match those of the previous day. These voice-overs will be used to link the footage of the area, giving the programme its seamless flow.

▲ On Wednesday morning the crew rapidly unload their equipment from the back of the estate car. They start work at 8am, taking a variety of shots of the locality to link the 'pieces to camera' ('PTCs') that Hugh will do later in the day.

◄ Sound engineer John Biddlecombe attaches the microphone to the inside of Hugh's overcoat before he prepares to do the first 'PTC'. Time is the enemy, especially towards the end of the year when the light begins to fade by mid-afternoon.

▲ 'And three … two … one' – as the director brings down his arm, Hugh begins his 'PTC'. He will do several 'takes', and each will be slightly different; the one for transmission will be chosen during editing.

▲ Time for the team to take a few minutes to check the camera angle on the monitor. Left to right: sound engineer John Biddlecombe, assistant cameraman Richard Smith, director Pete Smith, Hugh Scully, cameraman Chris Senior (kneeling).

▶ The camera crew set up the lightweight tracking and dolly on an even piece of ground. The camera, mounted on a tripod, sits on a length of wood that moves from side to side on two parallel poles. Filming in this way creates a greater depth of vision than a zoom lens can achieve and gives a good sense of the geography of a location.

▲ Open and at the ready, the steel lighting flight case holds the small pieces of vital equipment needed by the cameraman and his assistant as they move from place to place.

▲ The cameraman looks at his view finder but the director needs to be able to refer to a monitor while setting up a shot. The shield stops the sun reflecting on the screen.

▲ Hugh and the team may have to do several 'takes' before they can pack up the equipment and drive on to the next location. Deciding exactly where to go in advance makes for a smooth-running afternoon. Indecision could result in precious time being wasted.

The furniture round

Six weeks before the day of the *Roadshow* the team in Bristol invite members of the public to send in photographs and descriptions of objects too heavy to carry or bring by car. Posters are dispatched, and local radio and newspapers given every last detail. As the weeks pass the letters trickle in, and very often a stream becomes a flood. Up to 200 individual responses are allocated to transparent folders to create the furniture file.

Choosing the pieces that will be brought in for designer John Bone to arrange on the set, and then getting them safely to the venue, is a feat requiring military precision and, by the eleventh hour, almost split-second timing. On the Friday before the show, one of the team of furniture specialists arrives at the location, meets up with an assistant producer or director and is handed the weighty file. The careful process of selection begins.

During an action-packed three days, the pair make some 60 visits to homes in the area, looking not just at furniture, but also at clocks, sculpture, paintings and porcelain. The set would look very dull without a few good, decorative pieces to set it off, and these are in many cases spotted on the furniture round. In fact, an expert's eye is quite often caught by interesting and valuable objects that the owners themselves have never thought worth considering. Of course, the truth about such pieces is never revealed until the day of the show.

The mobile telephone has transformed the furniture round, making it far more flexible. Appointments can now be made *en route* by whoever is reading the map, whereas previously an entire day had to be planned in advance by telephoning from the hotel. Nevertheless, the hotel bedroom still doubles up as office and makeshift headquarters for the week.

By Tuesday morning it's time to make a final decision about the pieces to be brought in, contact the owners to arrange collection and liaise with the removal firm. Tough decisions have to be made; often pieces are rejected simply because they fall outside a route that will allow the collections to be made in one day.

At 8am on Wednesday the expert is in the cab of the furniture lorry – the director or assistant producer follows in a car – and they move off to the first pickup (the removal firm is not allowed to have the pickup list). By 4pm they must be at the venue with a full load, while at every stop pieces must be carefully wrapped and handled and the necessary paperwork completed (a full condition report for each item) before the journey can continue.

Executive producer Christopher Lewis and the furniture expert for the event sift through the haul once the lorry has been unloaded, deciding which of the pieces are good enough to be filmed. Agreement is reached, and the set builders can begin to create the display that is the backdrop to every *Roadshow*. By Friday evening the process has been carried out in reverse. Every last object is back in place, and a relieved expert sets off for home.

▲ On the Friday evening before the show, expert Nicholas Mitchell takes a first look at the bulging furniture file. His task is to whittle it down to around 60 entries so that he and the director can make 20 visits each day on the furniture round. Before it gets too late, they make a batch of appointments for the following day.

▲ Nicholas is back on the road again, map-reading, updating the file and making phone calls. As he and the driver work against the clock to criss-cross an area about 50 miles in diameter, the maze of unfamiliar streets begins to make sense to them.

▲ Nicholas takes a careful look at a stylish Arts and Crafts sideboard. It's up to him to decide whether or not pieces are genuine, as well as whether they will combine to make an attractive display.

▶ After an exhausting day it's time to get down to the paperwork. The evening is spent sifting, eliminating, deciding on the strategy for the next day and catching up with owners who were not at home when telephoned.

▼ It's good humour all the way as Nicholas watches the removal men carefully carry a sideboard down the front steps to the lorry waiting to transport it to the venue.

▲ Steady as she goes. The removal men use lengths of strong, woven tape to lift heavy pieces of furniture. Once loaded into the lorry, such pieces are secured to the sides to prevent damage in transit.

▲ Expert Nicholas Mitchell has decided that the sideboard is well worth bringing in, along with several other attractive objects owned by the same person. One of them, a charming painting, will catch the eye of expert Peter Nahum on the day.

▲ Nicholas writes out a full condition report for the sideboard, just in case any damage is done to it while it is in the *Roadshow*'s care. The owner gives permission for the pieces to be taken in, and the BBC insures them for the entire period that they are away from home.

▼ Furniture experts Penny Brittain and Adam Bowett examine a bureau. They are looking for the hallmarks of quality construction or strong local interest, which will persuade them that it is worth filming.

▲ It can take at least an hour to unload the full lorry. Nicholas supervises the operation while executive producer Christopher Lewis and an expert wait eagerly to see what the latest furniture round will yield. On the other side of the lorry, the scenery has been set for the next day.

◀ Earlier on the furniture round Nicholas visited the house of the man who wrote in to say that he owned a Bugatti chair. Together they looked the unusual piece over as the owner told the story of how it came into his family. Nicholas knew that this was something that expert Paul Atterbury would be delighted to capture on film, and it was taken on the lorry along with the sideboard.

▶ Paul Atterbury and the owner of the chair discuss its great merits as the cameras roll. Designed in the late 19th century by Carlo Bugatti, of the famous Italian family, it is richly inlaid, with panels of vellum and beaten copper forming the back and sides. The owner's mother was asked by her wealthy employers to pick anything of her choice as a wedding present. She chose wisely – the chair is now worth £2,000.

▼ The sideboard and other large items picked up on the furniture round make a delightful background for camera shots, as well as fascinating discussion pieces. Behind them the public queue patiently, hidden from the camera's view.

On the day

By 7pm on the evening before a *Roadshow* a deathly hush falls over the set. The crew and production team melt away, and Alec Yirrell makes sure that the venue is secure and hands over to security for the night. The success of the event is now in the hands of the public. Nothing warms the heart of executive producer Christopher Lewis more than the sight of a healthy queue forming when he arrives at around 8.30 the following morning.

The camera crews, TVOs, riggers, front-of-house manager and recording manager meet Christopher at the venue a good half hour before the rest of the team are called for 9am. Many members of the public prove their enthusiasm by starting their wait during the early hours of the morning. At Cleethorpes, in 1991, the first customer arrived at 4.30 in the morning, and it is not uncommon for people to be found patiently waiting at 7am.

At some point in the previous evening Christopher Lewis talks to a number of the experts – especially the furniture specialist, who will have seen the pieces come in on the lorry – to try to select one or two starting items for the main camera unit. The public is invited to move into the hall at 9.45am, so that, as recording begins, there are enough people on the set to create the bustling atmosphere that is an essential part of the *Roadshow*. If the filming schedule is looking sparse at 10 in the morning, one or two experts walk down the queue – it's never long before a few interesting objects come to light.

From 10am until 7pm, three main cameras record one item after another. A fourth camera, kept in the production room and known as the 'macro', is used for close-ups and small details. Hallmarks on silver, or the details on a watch or a piece of jewellery, can be filmed separately and edited in seamlessly for the finished programme. When a history of antiques programmes is written, the *Roadshow* will be remembered for pioneering the close-up – the viewer is never told something about an object and then frustrated by being unable to see it clearly.

Two directors work on the main unit in rotation. While one sits in the scanner during the recording of two or three items, the other talks to the recording manager about what is coming up so that they can discuss with the relevant expert how to approach particular objects. Nothing is rehearsed, but it is often useful to know what is going through the specialist's mind, and it can also help the expert to organize his or her thoughts. The piece will not be discussed with the owner lest a vital scrap of information should slip out prematurely and spoil the moment of revelation – it is important that the reaction of the owner is genuine. The director may also talk to the engineering manager or designer in case a piece needs lighting or dressing in a particular way.

In the production room, which is often set up in an equipment store or another secluded corner, either Christopher Lewis or Michèle Burgess views the proceedings on monitors. At the flick of a switch they can talk to the director in the scanner, where the sound supervisor and vision engineers also sit, looking after the sound controls and the colour and contrast on the camera exposures.

If you've ever attended a *Roadshow* and watched an item being filmed, you'll noticed that the expert and the owner continue to sit together for a while after the main conversation is over. This is when the 'noddies' (the endearing term for shots of the owner listening to the expert), additional close-up shots of the objects and retakes, which will all be of use during editing, are done.

▲ It's the early bird that catches the worm. Some of the team of experts arrive at the hall at the start of what promises to be a long and busy day.

▲ Patience is a great virtue, as anyone who has queued at the *Roadshow* will tell you.

Often there is a healthy line forming by 9am, but the wait is always worth it.

▲ Front-of-house manager Alec Yirrell directs his team of local helpers outside the hall.

▲ The queuing isn't over yet, but the reception area provides a welcome break. Here expert Margie Cooper takes a first look at the contents of all those precious packages.

▼ Before long the floor around every table is a sea of bubble wrap, crumpled newspaper and tea towels.

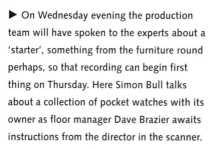

▲ A final test of the cameras that are to be used during the day takes place just before the public come in. The photograph of the girl is used as a continuity tool, to ensure that the adjustments in colour and tone on every camera remain the same from location to location.

▶ On Wednesday evening the production team will have spoken to the experts about a 'starter', something from the furniture round perhaps, so that recording can begin first thing on Thursday. Here Simon Bull talks about a collection of pocket watches with its owner as floor manager Dave Brazier awaits instructions from the director in the scanner.

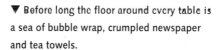

▲ It may look like a milling throng, but, while the public enjoy their day, detailed forward planning will have ensured that the team know what's expected of them.

▲ Floor assistant John Curry, a *Roadshow* veteran of 21 years, admires a vase while reassuring a customer that she is standing in the right queue – it just happens to be a long one. John's skills in queue management and diplomacy have been honed since the pilot programme was recorded in Hereford in May 1977.

▲ A borrowed shopping trolley provides the perfect method of transporting a collection of heirlooms. The wrappings and containers that are used to get precious objects to and from the *Roadshow* undamaged are sometimes as remarkable as the antiques themselves.

◀ Hilary Kay's expertise encompasses a long list of collecting categories – from dolls, teddies and rock-and-roll memorabilia to scientific instruments, mechanical music and automata. Here she examines a technical drawing set while another customer waits for her comments on an Abbey Road LP.

▲ Doll and teddy bear expert Bunny Campione enlists the help of ceramics expert Lars Tharp when a blue-and-white porcelain tea bowl and saucer turn up on her table.

▶ Penny Brittain certainly knows quality when she sees it. She made a bee-line for this Georgian *secretaire* bookcase when it arrived with the furniture round and now explains its merits to the proud owners in front of the cameras.

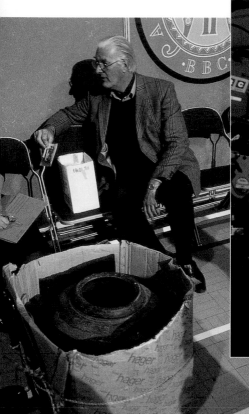

▲ After the owner's patient wait, ceramics expert John Sandon has plenty of interesting facts to tell him about his Roman amphora.

▶ Interesting, very interesting – silver and jewellery expert James Collingridge gives a small piece the third degree.

▼ The crew on the main camera unit prepare to record another piece of furniture. Behind the scenes, the lighting and the sound are being constantly monitored.

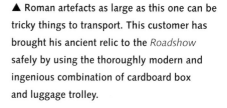

▲ Roman artefacts as large as this one can be tricky things to transport. This customer has brought his ancient relic to the *Roadshow* safely by using the thoroughly modern and ingenious combination of cardboard box and luggage trolley.

▲ You have been chosen! When an expert spots an object worth filming, the recording manager takes the customer to her desk, slots that person into the busy recording schedule and asks for permission to keep the piece locked in the security room until the moment of truth arrives.

▶ In the waiting room, comfortable chairs and a constant supply of hot drinks and sandwiches make the wait a little less nerve-racking.

▶ It's star treatment all the way as the customer goes to be made up before appearing in front of the cameras.

▼ The microphone is discreetly attached before the conversation between owner and expert, the essence of the *Antiques Roadshow*, begins.

▲ As the cameras roll, the history of an object is revealed. Owner and expert exchange information until that magical moment arrives when it's time for the expert to ask: 'Have you ever thought what your piece might be worth?'

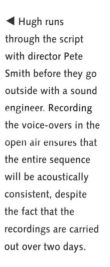

◄ Hugh runs through the script with director Pete Smith before they go outside with a sound engineer. Recording the voice-overs in the open air ensures that the entire sequence will be acoustically consistent, despite the fact that the recordings are carried out over two days.

▲ Hugh Scully finds a quiet place to set up his laptop computer and write the links that, with the pieces filmed on location the day before the show, form the opening sequence of every programme.

▼ Is it a watercolour or a print? Expert Rupert Maas explains various techniques to the owner while identifying the piece.

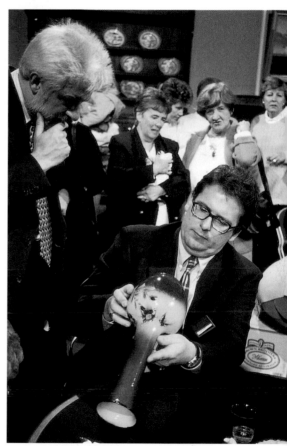

▲ One of the great advantages of attending the *Roadshow* is being able to listen to the experts exchanging views and knowledge. Here, Keith Baker asks Lars Tharp for his opinion on a long-necked vase.

◄ Experts and crew take a few minutes' welcome break to bolt down some lunch before rushing back to the set.

▶ Many of the experts work for leading auction houses and can get a second opinion when the need arises. Tim Wonnacott consults headquarters about a fine musical instrument.

▲ The portable single camera ('PSC') moves about the hall throughout the day, capturing those relaxed, chatty exchanges between owners and experts that have become an essential part of every *Roadshow*.

▶ Many visitors to the events are confirmed 'potaholics'. Expert Rosemary Bandini (right) works her way through a large, mixed collection of pieces.

▼ Bunny Campione holds a porcelain beauty in the sitting position to lend her some dignity in front of the camera, before laying her face-down to examine the mould number on the nape of her neck.

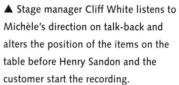

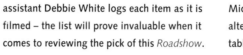

▲ Michèle Burgess at the vision desk in the scanner, directing the cameraman and stage manager in the hall. To her right, production assistant Debbie White logs each item as it is filmed – the list will prove invaluable when it comes to reviewing the pick of this *Roadshow*.

▲ Stage manager Cliff White listens to Michèle's direction on talk-back and alters the position of the items on the table before Henry Sandon and the customer start the recording.

▼ Whether you're queuing to get into the hall, or patiently sitting in the waiting room, there's no need to feel shut out from the action unfolding in front of the cameras. Strategically placed monitors relay the filming as it takes place.

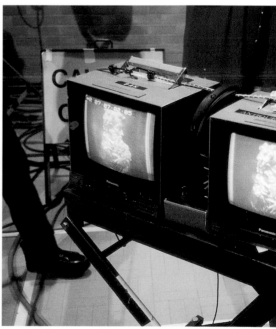

▲ Even on the *Antiques Roadshow* there are sometimes quiet moments. Stage manager Dave Brazier and the main camera crew wait for instructions to begin filming.

▶ Few visitors go home without a souvenir of the event. The *Roadshow* shop does a brisk trade all day.

▼ The shop's best-seller – a pile of 'I've queued at the *Antiques Roadshow*' badges lie waiting to be claimed.

▲ Cameraman Chris Senior, directed by Pete Smith on the right, records Hugh Scully's closing broadcast while there is still a fair-sized crowd in the hall. Hugh discusses the day's events with the producer before deciding what he will say.

▶ The doors close to the public at 4pm, but latecomers are often seen. Alec Yirrell, front-of-house manager and himself an experienced antiques dealer, takes the time to look at a young collector's treasure trove.

▲ After the unpacking comes the wrapping-up again. It's trying to fit it all back into the same space for the journey home that tends to prove difficult.

▲ Filming continues until 7pm, by which time the crowds have gone and the slightest noise is greatly magnified. As the last items are filmed the stage manager calls for quiet, and the experts speak as if recording in a full hall. Crowd noise is then added during editing to maintain continuity. Final pieces are recorded on the 'night set', when the main camera unit moves into a corner closer to the walls. When the programme is transmitted, the audience can't tell that the people have melted away.

▲ Long after the crowds have disappeared home, the riggers will still be hard at work dismantling the set. By 11pm the components of the *Roadshow* are stacked up against the walls, ready to be carried to the lorries first thing the next morning.

▲ Show me the way home. An exhausted but contented group of experts (left to right, Hilary Kay, Paul Atterbury and Tim Wonnacott) take their leave of another *Roadshow*. It is, as they say, 'a wrap'.

Editing for broadcast

When the team leave the location to return to base, they take with them a pile of videotapes holding many hours' worth of material. Between 23 and 25 items will have been recorded by the main camera unit, and around the same number by the roving PSC. Now begins the long process of editing the footage down to 18 to 20 items, each of no longer than two to four minutes' duration, to create a lively, fast-moving 45-minute programme.

The first stage is the 'paper edit', so called because one of the directors views all the material in a small room off the main office (and often takes videotapes home in the evening), making handwritten notes (on paper, hence the name) of what needs to be cut or saved. The tapes show a digital timecode at the edge of the screen, so exact sections can be identified.

After three to four days of this laborious process, two working weeks are spent in the off-line edit suite, dipping in and out of all the footage, keeping the good material and cutting other sections. Eventually the videotape ('VT') editor and director, working together, are left with

the basic shape of a programme that has pace, a good strong item to get the ball rolling, and all the separate pieces of Hugh Scully's opening sequence in order.

In the past, off-line editing involved running the tapes forwards and back to make the cuts, but the entire process is now done in a fraction of the time on computer, using a digital copy of the footage stored on disk. After two days, when the footage has been cut down to around 60 minutes, executive producer Christopher Lewis views the first cut and discusses with the director and VT editor which items can be dropped and which should be saved for one of the entertaining compilation programmes.

Once the footage has been cut to the right length the VT editor begins to put in the cutaways (close-ups), taking care not to disrupt the programme's continuity. This painstaking process of covering the joins and creating a seamless recording is highly skilled and takes until the end of the second week. Off-line editing yields a computer disk containing digital details of the order and duration of every shot to

be included. The disk is used in the on-line edit suite; here computer-controlled videotape players find the required shots from the original master tapes and copy or 'conform' them in the correct order onto the transmission tape.

The director emerges from on-line editing with a picture-perfect programme, complete with opening titles and credits, but with imperfect sound. At this point the programme goes to dubbing for the sound to be improved. Crowd noise is added, and unwanted sounds – excessive coughing and babies crying – are taken out, until, after six to eight hours, only one vital stage remains to be completed.

For 'layback', the new sound is literally laid back onto the transmission tape. Walk in on this process and you will find many bodies in a very small room, all furiously taking notes – this is the last opportunity to spot and correct less obvious mistakes such as little 'flashes' or visual errors. It's a moment of great relief when, after a final technical review, the *Roadshow* tape is signed and dispatched to BBC Television Centre in London, ready for transmission.

▲ In this small room off the main office the so-called 'paper edit' takes place, during which one of the directors views all the tapes brought back from the *Roadshow* and makes notes of possible cuts.

▲ Editor Vincent Wright (left) works alongside director Steve Wood (right) in the off-line edit suite on the next stage, which takes a full two weeks to complete.

▶ Appropriate music is chosen for the opening sequence of each programme. As one of the team of directors, Steve Potter is responsible for making a selection from the extensive music library, one of the great resources of the BBC.

▼ Videotape editor Steve Olive completes work on one of the compilation programmes in the on-line edit suite; here the shows are transferred from master tape onto transmission tape.

▲ A small selection of the *Roadshow* videotapes stored at BBC Bristol is proof of its long-running success.

◀ Several members of the production team crowd into the room during layback, when the sound is laid back onto the transmission tape. The more people who view at this stage, the greater the chance of picking up any remaining errors. In an effort to minimize the chance of those present missing anything, blinking is discouraged!

Overseas Roadshows

A successful television formula will always attract the attention of programme makers throughout the world. Small wonder then that the *Antiques Roadshow* was closely studied by producers in various countries as ratings soared year after year and fresh series were made.

In the late 1980s executive producer Christopher Lewis was approached by Swedish television executives from Malmö who were interested in developing the *Roadshow* format for Sweden. A deal was struck, not just with the Swedes, but with Danish television as well. As a result the first two programmes to be made abroad were recorded in 1989 and included in series 12, one of them broadcast from Sweden and the other from Denmark. Nowadays, under licence from the BBC, the Swedes produce their own, highly popular, version.

The Swedish and Danish shows, with their tantalizing variety of objects and a foreign location, were also well received in Britain and whetted the viewers' appetite for more. In Scandinavia the team gained the experience that would prove valuable when the time came to set up *Roadshows* in places such as Amsterdam, Arras and Brussels. 'It was our first experience of interpreting by earpiece,' said Christopher Lewis. 'An interpreter fed the translation through to the customer and the expert. There were slight pauses, but they were edited out later and it worked very well.'

The *Antiques Roadshow* must always be recorded in English for the British audience. Many approaches have been made by countries that would love the *Roadshow* to visit, but want it to be made in their own language; sadly, their requests must be politely turned down. What does work well, however, is to allow the public event to take place in the language of the hosts, but to carry out the recording in English. For example, when the *Roadshow* went to Brussels and Arras many of the experts were able to talk to the customers at the tables in French, but switched to English, assisted by interpreters, when the cameras rolled for the main items.

Of course language posed no problem in Malta, Gibraltar or Jamaica, but every new country has a habit of throwing up a variety of challenges. The Maltese, for instance, have a reputation for being very private people, and the fear was that they would not turn out on the day. Happily, the lure of the BBC and a team of world-renowned experts proved irresistible, and a jostling crowd bearing all manner of fascinating items streamed through the venue all day. In Jamaica a rumour suggesting that the BBC had come to buy from the islanders had to be extinguished as hastily as it had been ignited.

Logistics and practicalities are even more of an issue when the team travel abroad. At such times the best way to avoid difficulties and misunderstandings is to employ a trustworthy local 'fixer' – someone who can spot a problem before it happens. Even so, the best-laid plans …

For the Jamaican *Roadshow*, the outside broadcast equipment had to be packed in 50 reinforced travel cases and flown out ahead of most of the crew. Arrangements had been made for it to be unloaded and put into secure storage until it could be transported to the venue. When the flight arrived in the middle of the night and the ground staff did not appear, engineering manager John Neal and designer John Bone had to turn out in the small hours, unload each piece into a luggage trolley and find a safe place to store it overnight.

The co-production made with Swedish television, SVT, led to an error that called for some last-minute repainting. When the set arrived it was unveiled with great ceremony – to red faces all round. 'SVT' had become 'STV', the abbreviation for Scottish Television.

Despite the odd hiccup, the overseas *Roadshows* have proved a tremendous success, turning up treasures such as the album of Filipino paintings found in Brussels that later sold at Christie's in London for £250,000. The team would like to record a foreign event every year, provided that the necessary sponsorship is forthcoming. Australia, New Zealand, Canada, South Africa and Israel are among possible future locations, while the Japanese have also shown interest.

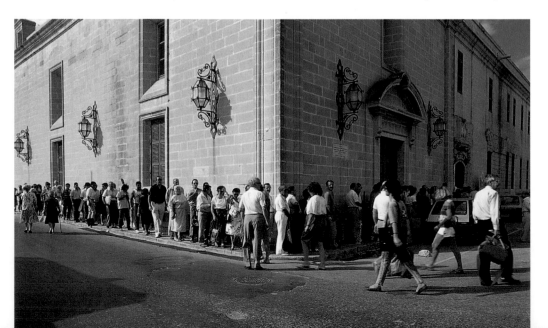

◀ St John's Hospital, Valletta, built by the Knights of St John at the end of the 16th century, provided a splendidly imposing setting for the *Roadshow* held in Malta in 1990. The experts were deluged with fascinating objects brought in by an enthusiastic crowd, who queued all day to find out about the history and value of their treasures.

▲ The weather was balmy and the scenic locations abundant. Hugh Scully stands at the water's edge in Malta to record a piece to camera. The island, 58 miles southwest of Sicily and filled with Baroque architecture, has long been a magnet for the British.

► Negotiating the narrow streets of Malta, which are lined with stone houses containing a wealth of fine pictures and furniture, proved tricky. The lorry eventually arrived at the location, where local helpers unloaded the furniture and pictures stowed inside.

▼ Not least among the items brought along to the event in Malta were several stunning pieces of jewellery, including this wide, solid-gold bangle. The piece is decorated with circular micro-mosaic panels, showing peasant figures, set into plaques of malachite.

▲ As the sun began to set behind the great rock of Gibraltar, the lorry containing the set – resplendent with the unmistakable logo of the *Antiques Roadshow* – arrived safely at this southernmost tip of Europe.

▼ These houses among the treetops in the Philippines are the subject matter of another of the Lozano watercolours (see right). The owner's grandfather, who commissioned the paintings, owned a cigar factory in Manila.

▶ This depiction of a group of rather dapper gentlemen is just one of the 25 watercolours by the artist José Honorato Lozano that were found by Peter Nahum at Brussels. They were in an album of valuable Filipino paintings that was later sold at auction, through Christie's, for the remarkable sum of £250,000.

Overseas Roadshows

Malmö, Sweden 1989
Helsingor, Denmark 1989
Valletta, Malta 1990
Kingston, Jamaica 1992
Gibraltar 1993
Brussels, Belgium 1995
Amsterdam, Netherlands 1996
Arras, France 1997

▲ It was a busy day at Reception – and a sweltering one, too, as the crowds thronged the open-air venue at Devon House in Kingston, Jamaica, for the fourth successful overseas event.

▼ People came from all over the island to Jamaica's *Roadshow*, the furthest afield that the team has ventured. They were given a warm welcome during several memorable days under Caribbean skies.

The Next Generation

Readers who are familiar with BBC1's energetic Saturday-morning children's programme, with its stream of guests, comedy acts and audience participation, might remember that in the early 1990s it was called *Going Live*. The presenters at the time were Phillip Schofield and Sarah Greene.

One celebrity guest during this period was the *Antiques Roadshow*'s Hilary Kay, who, as Head of Sotheby's Collectors' Division, brought along a selection of rock and pop memorabilia to show the audience. The response to Hilary's appearance was overwhelming, and so the producers at *Going Live* began talking enthusiastically to their counterparts on the *Roadshow* in Bristol.

Why not, it was decided, put on a children's show that would encourage young people's interest in collecting? Ask any number of the experts on the *Roadshow* when they began to appreciate antiques and you'll find they started at an early age. As children they squirrelled away drawers full of stamps, conkers, coins and cigarette cards, only to begin specializing and accumulating detailed knowledge as adults.

The shows are now an annual event, each taking place at an unusual venue with attractions to hold the attention of the children and provide an entertaining, action-packed day out for the family. There is an hourly quiz, with winners announced over the PA system, and a competition for viewers that goes out on air. A celebrity presenter, well known to the children, works with Hugh Scully throughout the day.

Unlike the *Antiques Roadshow*, for which the public often queue for several hours, the children's shows are ticketed and divided into morning and afternoon sessions to minimize waiting. When the forthcoming event is advertised nationally, children who respond are sent application forms so that the production team have an idea of what will be coming in. Greater emphasis is placed on collections put together by the children themselves than on valuable individual items.

The children's excitement at being part of the event shines through and is highly infectious. It's refreshing for the experts to talk to visitors who are less concerned with money than with enjoying amassing a collection that has a more personal value. The hope of the experts is that their own enduring love of antiques will inspire the young collectors who visit these *Roadshows* to become the connoisseurs of tomorrow.

▲ Three attentive listeners gather round one of the ceramics tables to listen to David Battie explain the date and origins of their dish.

▲ Henry Sandon is completely potty – teapotty, that is. Like so many of the experts chosen for the annual children's show, he makes a special effort to dress appropriately, and for Henry there is nothing quite so appropriate as a pot, in whatever form.

▲ The children's *Roadshow* is a great day out. With so much going on, there is plenty to keep everyone occupied, even those with the shortest attention span. The locations are carefully chosen, and in the event of the children becoming bored with watching the process of making the programme, there are other activities to keep them entertained.

◀ Floor manager Dave Brazier co-ordinates the process of recording an object. Wired for sound, he can talk to the director in the scanner and relay instructions to expert Geoffrey Munn waiting with the children.

▲ 'This is the trouble with show business,' Geoffrey Munn explains to the girls. 'All the hanging about on set, doing take after take until the director gets just what he wants.' He's joking of course – spontaneity is as important at the children's *Roadshows* as it is at the 'adult' events.

◀ 'How much would you put on this very fragrant and appealing bundle, produced only a matter of weeks ago?' Bunny Campione asks colleague Hugo Marsh. His verdict? 'Well, he's part of the Next Generation, so I would say he's priceless – and well worth hanging on to.'

◀ Book and manuscript expert Clive Farahar shares a young owner's enthusiasm for her huge collection of Rupert Bear books. Her grandfather knew Alfred Bestell, the illustrator. On the endpaper of one of the volumes, Bestell has made a small drawing of a church with Mount Snowdon behind it.

▲ Toy expert Justin Pressland bends down to look closely at an example of 'Dinah', an American cast-iron mechanical money bank manufactured by John Harper. Fakes abound, so close scrutiny is essential.

▲ Silver and jewellery expert Ian Harris explains the significance of this young man's Jewish spice tower.

▲ Floor manager Dave Brazier adjusts his earpiece as he listens to the director speaking to him from the scanner. It's almost time to start recording the next item, and this time Hugh Scully joins toy expert Justin Pressland and the young owner at the table.

◀ 'Thunderbirds are go!' The popular 1960s television series now enjoys cult status. Dinky produced models of Thunderbird 2 and Lady Penelope's FAB 1 in the late 1960s. This is a more recent vintage, a Tracy Island toy issued in 1992 by Vivid Imaginations. It became one of those 'must have' Christmas presents of the year. The proud owner shows his off to Hugo Marsh.

▲ What do you think of it so far? Expert Paul Atterbury and daughter Zoe, now a veteran helper on the children's shows, spend a few minutes catching up on the day's events during a quiet spell on reception.

▲ Everyone needs a little help from their friends. Natalie Harris and Philip Taubenheim drop some hints about the answers to a few of the questions posed by the hourly quiz.

▼ There's nothing like a touch of healthy competition to add some spice to the proceedings. Alec Yirrell announces the winners of the latest hourly quiz, with the help of his right-hand woman, Zoe Atterbury.

▶ Over the years she's hunted for them high and low, but it's all been worth it just for this moment. The proud owner of a vast collection of badges holds them up for all to see.

▼ Collecting autographs is a favourite passion among children, and the team of *Roadshow* experts sign countless pieces of paper during the day. Eric Knowles executes a deadly accurate self-portrait alongside his signature. His son, Oliver (right), sticks close to Dad to learn the ropes.

▼ Clive Stewart-Lockhart and Hilary Kay admire the books and prints brought in by one of the older visitors.

Children's Roadshows

BRISTOL 1991, Brunel Centre. *Presenters*: Phillip Schofield, Sarah Greene, Gordon the Gopher.

YORK 1992, National Railway Museum. *Presenters*: Anthea Turner, Kristian Schmidt (Todd in *Neighbours*), Andi Peters and Michaela Strachan.

LONDON 1993, Science Museum. *Presenters*: Anthea Turner, Andi Peters.

MANCHESTER 1994, Granada Studios Tour. *Presenter*: Emma Forbes.

BELFAST 1995, Ulster Folk and Transport Museum. *Presenter*: Diane-Louise Jordan.

EDINBURGH 1996, Royal Museum of Scotland. *Presenter*: Sally Gray.

CARDIFF 1997, Techniquest. *Presenter*: Philippa Forrester.

▲ Gather round, everybody. Hugh Scully and Philippa Forrester get all the cheering on they need as dozens of willing volunteers help them to bid the viewers goodbye from Techniquest, Cardiff, the site of the seventh triumphant children's *Roadshow*.

An overwhelming response...

Every day a flood of letters arrives at the *Roadshow*'s production office in Bristol. 'I'm happy to say that, with only one or two exceptions, all are very complimentary,' says executive producer Christopher Lewis. In line with BBC policy, every correspondent receives a reply.

Many people write to say 'thank you' after visiting a *Roadshow* because they enjoyed the day and felt that they were part of the making of the programme, which indeed they were. Other people write to say that they own, say, a piece of furniture, a vase or a painting almost identical to one shown on the programme. Not everyone is seeking a valuation –

which, in any case, the BBC cannot provide – but simply have a snippet of additional information to pass on, such as a family connection with an artist or potter. Many people spot a piece in the background – often an object that was picked up on the furniture round and was used to dress the set – and want to establish exactly what it is because they have one like it.

Roadshow fans also write asking when the team will next be visiting their area, while some suggest venues. Unsurprisingly, many of the letters are addressed to Hugh Scully, who, as the *Roadshow*'s presenter, has been its reassuring anchor for many years. 'I think our postbag tells us that we

are very much a part of people's lives,' says Christopher Lewis. 'By writing to us, viewers and visitors make a connection with the programme that is as important to them as it is to us.'

The *Antiques Roadshow* has often been the subject of sketches and jokes in other television programmes and of cartoons in newspapers and magazines. It provides a rich vein of material for comedy writers who often use it to draw parallels with other well-known British institutions – from the royal family to the National Health Service – and as a familiar feature of modern life it is sure to be the source of much merriment in the future.

"Ahh! A hospital bed! Now I haven't seen one of these for a very long time"

◄ Presenter Hugh Scully (left) with executive producer Christopher Lewis, who holds the BAFTA award won by the *Antiques Roadshow*: the Lew Grade Award for a Significant and Popular Programme, 1995.

▲ *The Times* 19 November 1997.

◄ *The Daily Telegraph* 27 July 1995.

► *Private Eye* 4 October 1996.

▼ *Evening Standard* 21 June 1996.

"You'll be pleased to hear that it's the Holy Grail. Have you got it insured?"

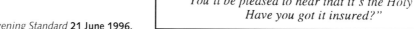

▲ *The Guardian* **19 October 1993.**

▶ *The Spectator* **9 May 1998.**

◀ *Radio Times* **2–8 April 1988.**

▼ *Sunday Mirror* **2 February 1992.**

▲ Most viewers' letters offer additional information on a piece, congratulate the experts on their knowledge, suggest a future venue or simply thank everybody responsible for the pleasure they have given over the years. Whatever the subject, together they add up to a full postbag every day of the week.

▶ Two-year-old border collie Bonnie from Yorkshire is a dog with extremely good taste. Every Sunday, as the *Antiques Roadshow* theme tune begins, she sits in front of the television, head erect, and 'sings' along to the music.

The Great Finds

◀ It's definitely a Bugatti. Paul Atterbury and the owner of a piece found on the 'furniture round' discuss its history and how it came into the owner's possession.

Over the years the *Roadshow* has asked the nation to turn out its broom cupboards, its attics and even its garden sheds. The public has obliged, and the rewards have been rich and plentiful. During 20 series, almost four million objects have been valued, totalling a notional value of £200 million.

On the following pages you can read about some of the great finds that made the headlines and changed the lives of their owners. From humble pottery to fabulous works of art thought to be lost to the world, many of these pieces have long been treasured by their owners, while others were considered worthless until that magical moment when, as the cameras rolled, the truth was revealed.

English marquetry commode

Found in Douglas, 1984; valued at over £30,000. Current value up to £80,000.

Penny Brittain was in charge of the furniture round on the Isle of Man in 1984. She made an appointment to call at a farmhouse, and when she arrived found herself caught up in the aftermath of a silver-wedding party. 'There were geese in the kitchen and presents everywhere,' she said. 'Underneath one pile I saw the commode. They didn't rate it at all, but I couldn't believe my eyes. The mother had been in service and had been left it when one of the family died.'

The Isle of Man commode, as the piece is always described today, turned out to be of remarkable significance. 'It is the most important piece that I have ever done on the *Roadshow*,' said John Bly, 'an English George III bombé marquetry commode made around 1773 in the French style. We cannot attribute it to one particular maker, but there were half-a-dozen men working at that time who might have produced it or who might have closely instructed a pupil to do the work.' The commode was later sold at Sotheby's and subsequently at Asprey for £50,000.

The quality of the marquetry was superb. When new the piece would have been brightly coloured, but time had faded the harewood (sycamore dyed green), the satinwood and the various other natural and dyed pieces of timber that formed the ribbons, flowers and leaves.

The construction was wonderful. 'The drawers were immediately on top of one another,' said John. 'In other words there was no intersecting strip of carcass between them. The ormolu mounts were also worth noting. Only traces of the original gilding were left, and the detail was blunted by dirt and polish, but beneath that you could see just how finely chiselled they were.'

Another feature was the technique used to give detail to the marquetry. 'On 17th-century marquetry the details such as the veins on leaves and the feathery quality on petals was done by cutting through the veneers with a very fine saw. In the 18th century, however, the details were etched and did not penetrate the veneers, so time wears away some of the original sharp definition, as was the case on this example.'

18th-century cabinet makers

England's cabinetmaking trade was given a tremendous boost towards the end of the 17th century. From 1685, after the Revocation of the Edict of Nantes, many Huguenot craftsmen in wood fled religious persecution in France and settled in London. Then, in 1689, a Dutch King, William III, came to the English throne and Dutch and German cabinet makers moved to England to practise their craft. Cross-fertilization between their techniques and those of indigenous craftsmen resulted in the production of many fine examples of marquetry furniture for some of the finest houses in the country. By the late 18th century, when the piece shown here was made, the skills of the English cabinet maker were very well honed. Men such as John Cobb, who died in 1778, and his partner William Vile made furniture for the Royal Household; so too did Pierre Langlois, a Frenchman who eventually adopted the name Peter Langley.

William Kent-style table

Found in Colchester, 1994; valued at £15,000. Current value the same.

Extraordinary though it may seem, this magnificent side table was spotted by its present owner in a Hampshire junk shop over 40 years ago. It carried a price tag of £60 – a lot of money in the 1950s – and he was unable to afford it at the time. When he returned the following year the table was still there, so he snapped it up.

And an exceptional investment it turned out to be. Furniture expert Deborah Lambert spent some time examining it when it was unloaded from the lorry on the afternoon before the *Roadshow*. 'It was made c.1730–40 in the style of William Kent, whose ideas and designs were so influential during that period,' she said. 'The detailed carved base is pine and the top marble. Originally the wood would have been richly gilded, but that has completely worn off over the years.'

Although Kent's influence is obvious, the table, which would once have graced a large country house, was not made under his direction. 'If you look at the very best Kent furniture in somewhere like Houghton Hall in Norfolk,' said Deborah, 'you will see that the sphinxes are perfectly proportioned, whereas these have huge heads and matronly busts which lead down to very puny hindquarters. Kent was known for his massive side tables with carved supports modelled as eagles with outstretched wings, but this bird has a sort of swan's head and neck and an eagle's wings and feet.'

The table may have an Egyptianesque look, but, said Deborah, it was inspired more by Ancient Rome. 'When they excavated Nero's Golden House in the 15th century they discovered frescos depicting figures that combined human, plant and animal forms. Raphael copied them during the Renaissance and then Jean Bérain in the 17th century, and they went on to be used in a much larger form in the 18th century.'

William Kent

One of the most important English protagonists of the Palladian style of architecture during the first half of the 18th century was William Kent (1684–1748). Palladianism, a rigid version of the classical style of Ancient Rome, was based on the designs of the Renaissance Italian architect Andrea Palladio (1508–80). As well as being an architect, William Kent was a landscape gardener, an interior decorator and a furniture designer. After studying for several years in Italy he met Richard Boyle, the third Earl of Burlington, who became his patron and employer. To furnish the new Palladian houses Kent designed a wide variety of objects in a complementary heavy, classical style, including cabinets, mirror frames, chairs, beds and console tables. Kent's work was highly influential and was copied by many of the most celebrated cabinet makers of the day.

Pair of Neo-classical demi-lune tables

Found in Hemel Hempstead, 1991; valued at £70–80,000 the pair. Current value £100–120,000.

Christopher Payne still eulogizes about this pair of demi-lune tables, which were made c.1770–75. 'They are without doubt among the finest examples of English furniture I have ever seen at a *Roadshow*,' he said.

'They were quite big for tables of this type,' Christopher went on, 'and it is very rare to come across a pair. Although often made in pairs, most have been separated over the years as large houses were sold and their contents dispersed. They are quite typical of the period in this very formal, restrained Neo-classical style that was well established by 1770.'

At the time Christopher thought that they could possibly have been made to an exact design by Robert Adam, but it is now thought too contentious to attribute pieces of this kind specifically. Certainly they are very much in the Adam style and could have been made in the workshops of a number of eminent London cabinet makers of the time, such as William Ince and John Mayhew or John and William Linnell.

Known as pier or side tables, they would have been made to fit exactly the spaces (or piers) between the windows of a room. Often there were grand decorative mirrors above that filled the space and reflected light into the room from candelabra. The tables were considered an important part of the decoration of a room, and were either of satinwood, like these two, or giltwood.

Typically, these pieces are decorated with some of the classical motifs of the day, such as husks and anthemion (a radiating pattern resembling honeysuckle). Very early examples of feathering, done in boxwood, appeared to have been inked out, and the feathering seemed to have been done by penwork. The delicate inlay and the rich, contrasting tones of the surface indicated the work of the very best craftsmen.

The Adam style

There is no doubt that the influence of Robert Adam (1728–92) was to be found in every grand, redecorated and carefully integrated interior in England by the late 18th century. Adam was born in Kirkcaldy, Scotland, the son of William Adam (1689–1748), who was himself an eminent architect. In 1754 Robert went to Italy, where he studied and absorbed every aspect of ancient design and ornament. When he returned to England after four years he embarked on his highly successful career as an architect – by 1762 he had become the sole architect to George III. In 1773, with his brother James (1730–94), Adam began publishing a series of engravings of his designs. Apart from public buildings, he designed town houses and great country estates. He died the most fashionable architect of the 18th century and was buried in Westminster Abbey.

Painted Pembroke table

Found in Cleethorpes, 1991; valued at £25,000. Current value up to £35,000.

When John Bly walked into the hall at Cleethorpes on Wednesday afternoon after the furniture lorry had been unloaded, this was the very first piece that caught his eye. The pretty, elegant little satinwood Pembroke table had been in the owner's family for 40 years. The owner himself had been given the table by his grandmother, to whom had it been presented as a gift when she was working in Maidenhead as a lady's companion.

John's first task was to confirm that the piece was from the late 18th century, rather than one of the mass-produced versions of this type of table that appeared in the late 19th century. Next he examined the painted decoration on its surface very closely. Many plain tables of this kind were painted a hundred years or so later, or even early in the 20th century, and appearances can be extremely deceptive.

Every aspect John looked at confirmed his initial instinct that the table was 'right', from the three hand-made steel screws and the handsaw marks to the crystallization that was present on the timber. It was clear from each of these characteristics that no machine had been involved at any stage in the table's construction.

There was additional evidence to point convincingly to the date of the table. The hinges fitted to its underside were rusted and the extensions supported by lopers, the last a feature not found on 19th-century tables of this type. Around the edge of the surface there was painting that complemented the natural figuring of the grain running across the frieze drawer and down the legs. The painting's depth and contrast indicated that the work had been carried out at the time the piece was made, rather than at any subsequent period, thus confirming its authenticity.

Pembroke tables

It was in the mid-18th century that household inventories first began to record the existence of Pembroke tables, so we must assume that the earliest examples were made at that time. The story goes that they were named after the Countess of Pembroke, who ordered a table to be made with four legs and with drop-leaves at either side, supported on lopers, so that when the table was fully opened it provided a small but useful surface (the surface could be round, oval or rectangular). The design chosen by the Countess was highly practical. The flaps could be dropped and the table pushed against the wall when it was not needed, and then brought out for breakfast or for taking tea during the day. These pieces, which can also be used as games or work tables, are still popular today, particularly in small houses and flats where space is at a premium.

Pair of Georgian dumb waiters

Found in Enniskillen, 1991; valued at £15,000 the pair. Current value up to £25,000.

To find one good Georgian dumb waiter at a *Roadshow* is cause for celebration, but it made John Bly's day to be presented with a matching pair. Made from a beautiful mahogany, they were glowing with the soft patina that had built up over two centuries.

This pair was made around 1785, with a swept tripod leg base that is very typical of the 1780s (mid-18th-century dumb waiters often have tripod bases with cabriole legs). John examined the pieces closely in order to reassure himself that the dumb waiters really were as good as they had appeared at first glance; he was looking for any evidence that they were not a perfect pair.

To his great satisfaction everything was perfectly in order. The tell-tale signs that he looked for were the colour underneath, the hand-made clout-nails, the slightly rough undersides (left that way because they were never intended to be seen), and the original casters finished with a mercurial gilding.

One of the most attractive features of this pair of dumb waiters was the columns between the three dished trays. The skilled turning of the columns, used to create the vase shapes, is the same all the way down each piece, simply becoming slightly larger in circumference until it meets the base. The work would have been executed using

a foot-operated lathe, which allowed the carver to chisel the wood into the required shape as it revolved.

Dumb waiters such as these examples were found in the most fashionable late-Georgian dining rooms. When the servants retired at the end of the meal (towards the end of the 18th century the hour at which dinner was taken had moved from 2–3pm to 5–6pm), the dumb waiters were placed at the corners of the dining table. They held wine, condiments, clean plates and cutlery, as well as other dining accessories, to enable those present to continue feasting without the inconvenience of rising from the table, or the intrusion of servants.

Dumb waiters

The dumb waiter was an English invention, introduced around 1740, with a design based on the tripod table. It usually consisted of three trays around a central column, graduated in size with the largest tray at the bottom and the smallest one at the top. Casters were often attached to the feet so that the dumb waiter could be moved easily. Later on, and further on into the Victorian period, rectangular and square dumb waiters were also made, as were more capacious versions that incorporated wine coolers and drum tables below. Dumb waiters were also designed with drop leaves so that they could lean against a wall when not in use. This type is not as popular with collectors today as the standard model with fixed trays. Since fixed trays have holes bored through their centres they are particularly vulnerable to splitting, and two-tier examples have sometimes been cut down as a result. As its name implies, the dumb waiter was intended to replace servants in situations where they might hear indiscreet, inebriated gossip and then broadcast it among their colleagues until it became common knowledge both above and below stairs. They were, therefore, made use of after the meal, when the ladies withdrew to the drawing room, the servants were dismissed, and the men remained in the dining room to drink toasts and debate.

Walnut veneer kneehole desk

Found in Berwick-Upon-Tweed, 1992; valued at £6,500. Current value £8–10,000.

Some very clever bargain-hunters have brought their finds to the *Roadshow* over the years, but the owner of this wonderful George II walnut kneehole desk must be one of the canniest and luckiest of them all. Shortly after getting married, the owner was living in a flat in Croydon when the elderly lady who lived next door rang the doorbell and asked her husband if he would help her carry a desk down the stairs ready to be carted away. 'She said that they would never agree to take it if she couldn't leave it outside the front door!' recalled the owner.

Fortunately, the newly-weds rescued the desk from its undignified fate, and the dustmen's loss was their gain. By the time the desk was brought to John Bly's attention it had been in the family for 32 years. Typical of the 18th century, the piece is veneered in walnut on a pine carcass, with drop-handles of cut brass loops attached to a pierced backplate. The original handles, which in this case survive, are particularly important to the value of a piece.

Anyone looking for a desk, reasonably small like this example and suited to small, modern living spaces, is spoilt for choice. The *bonheur du jour*, which is another development of the 18th century, and the Davenport are both good examples.

The *bonheur du jour* was designed with ladies in mind. The form varies, but usually incorporates a series of small drawers, a hinged writing lid or a pull-out surface, and a galleried top to hold novels or ornaments. The Davenport takes its name from Captain Davenport, who ordered the first one in the late 18th century. He wanted a small but commodious desk to take to India, and the design in its various forms, with drawers running down one side, dummy drawers down the other and a sloping desk above, has been highly popular ever since.

Kneehole desks

We take the design of the kneehole desk for granted, but examine one more closely and you will see that it looks just like a chest of drawers with a central hole. These desks were introduced at the start of the 18th century, in the reign of Queen Anne (1702–14). Originally intended as dressing-tables, they were soon used as ladies' writing desks. The kneehole desk is one of the oldest forms of flat-topped writing table, with one or two long drawers at the top, a recessed cupboard beneath the surface and narrow drawers on either side. The earliest examples were made of walnut or oak, followed by red walnut and then mahogany. By the mid-18th century, pedestal desks, with three separate sections (one for the top drawers and two for side drawers), had come into fashion. Six feet are more desirable than four, and drawer fronts of pine rather than oak are a good clue to authenticity.

The Arming of Telemachus

Found on the Wirral, 1996; valued at £25–35,000. Current value the same.

Although the *Roadshow* might be ground-breaking television, tearing down brick walls has not been part of the programme's style. Until, that is, the office received a call asking a representative to go to a lock-up garage where, they were assured, something of very great interest lay safely bricked up behind a wall.

It was too intriguing to resist and, as the wall came down, this handsome full-size marble sculpture was slowly revealed. The owner had found it in a stonemason's yard in 1978, black with dirt and covered by a flimsy shed. The business had closed, and the site was about to be turned into a car park. When the bulldozers moved in the statue was due to be crushed and used as hardcore. Not knowing what it was, the gentleman paid £300 for it and arranged for it to be moved.

Fearing theft or damage, he bricked up the statue in 1982. Certain parts of it were missing, but the owner, who had carried out a considerable amount of research on the piece, had them made in plaster, taken from the original model kept at St Luke's in Rome.

The Arming of Telemachus was carved from the very best white Carrara marble in 1835. It is the work of the Italian sculptor Luigi Bienaimé (1795–1878), who became the supervisor of the Rome studios of the Danish sculptor Bertel Thorvaldsen. Bienaimé was commissioned to produce the figure by a Prince Golitsin. It was first displayed in a palace in Russia before being moved to Eaton Hall, near Chester, where it stood with three other statues until 1885; how it came to rest in a stonemason's yard is still a mystery. The surface of the marble had been affected by exposure to damp over the years, but nonetheless it remains a fascinating and beautiful object.

19th-century Italian sculpture

The new classicism of the late 18th and early 19th centuries looked back to ancient Greece rather than to Rome for inspiration. Canova (1757–1822) was its greatest exponent, but Bertel Thorvaldsen (1768–1844), for whom Bienaimé worked, was a celebrated Danish sculptor and a leader of the international Neo-classical movement. Marble had been the main material used in ancient Greek architecture, and pure white Carrara marble was preferred to the coloured and patterned marbles used by Roman sculptors. It was quarried at Carrara and Petra Santa in Tuscany from the 3rd century BC, and the columns for the Pantheon and the Palace of Domitian, both built in Rome, were carved from it. Here it has been used to create the figure of Telemachus, son of Odysseus and Penelope.

Ferdinand Preiss figure

Found in Bexhill-on-Sea, 1994; valued at £8,000. Current value the same.

As a specialist in Art Nouveau and Art Deco, and one who particularly admires the sculpture of the period, Eric Knowles was delighted to come across such an impressive example of the work of the German Art Deco sculptor Ferdinand Preiss; the piece had been in the family of the owner's mother for many years. Made in the expensive combination of ivory and bronze known as 'chryselephantine', it displayed superb carving.

'There are so many fakes on the market today, made of resin in the Far East [see page 145], that it was a pleasure to come across one at a *Roadshow* that was so obviously genuine and in such good condition,' said Eric. 'The fakes have very badly finished bases with artificially rusted nuts and rods securing the figures to them. They also have dirt rubbed into the crevices and are usually of patinated metal rather than bronze.' The condition of the figure was also a pleasant surprise to Eric: 'The ball she is holding in the air is made of celluloid, a very brittle and vulnerable material, so it is remarkable that it survived intact.'

The piece, which was made between 1930 and 1936, was all the more unusual for two further reasons. First, the base was inscribed 'Ada May Lighter Than Air', and second, the embossed and gilt paper label put on before the piece left the foundry had survived. Preiss did not normally model his figures on real people. Ada May was a famous actress and dancer of the period who appeared in various productions put on by the renowned impresario C B Cochran. She obviously made a great impression on the artist, for, although Preiss did model actresses, he is more widely known for his sporting figures playing golf or skiing.

'Ada was standing on quite an elaborate stepped base – architectural in form and composed of different coloured marbles – which added slightly to her value. Plain bases of Brazilian green onyx, for instance, are slightly less desirable,' said Eric, 'but the value really lay in the quality of the figure. At the time, I can remember saying that I wished she lived on my mantelpiece!'

Ferdinand Preiss

Ferdinand Preiss (1882–1943) produced some of the most desirable Art Deco figures on the market today. 'His women don't have the theatrical qualities of the figures produced by other artists, such as Colinet or Chiparus,' said Eric. 'He went in for these eerily lifelike creatures, very Aryan and athletic in appearance, with anatomically correct facial features and limbs.' The ivory face was given a dainty wash of paint to make it even more realistic. Preiss's work was manufactured at the Preiss–Kassler Foundry in Berlin (pieces usually bear the 'PK' monogram), which was established in 1906. Preiss ceased production during the First World War, but resumed in 1919 and by 1929 had several designers working for him. Figures that appear to have been made by Preiss should be treated with caution. His work, because of its popularity, has been much copied, often using a softer stone and with over-elaborate bases.

Richard Dadd painting

Found in Barnstaple, 1986. Bought by the British Museum in 1987 for £100,000.

A large queue had already formed when fine art expert Peter Nahum arrived first thing in the morning. As he walked to his table he noticed in the queue a large painting packed between two pieces of cardboard; two hours later it was finally laid before him. It was to be one of the most important discoveries in the history of the *Roadshow*: a lost work by the British artist Richard Dadd, entitled *Artists Halt in the Desert*.

It is unlikely that any other expert would have recognized the painting for what it is. Peter had handled many other great Dadds at Sotheby's and felt very familiar with the artist and his work. The piece was unsigned, but carried a strange inscription in French on the back. The owners thought that it was, perhaps, a type of print. It had been hanging on their sitting-room wall, but they were about to put it in the garden shed while they redecorated the house.

Although Peter's instincts told him the artist was Dadd, he needed to do further research and consulted Patricia Allderidge, archivist and curator at the Bethlem Royal Hospital Museum in London. The Museum was formerly an asylum, and Dadd had

been incarcerated there after being certified insane in 1844. Peter's description led Patricia to believe that it could be one of three paintings recorded in cataloguing for an exhibition in 1857 and subsequently lost.

Once she had seen the work she was able to match it with the catalogue notes describing it as portraying travellers camping on the shores of the Dead Sea; it was probably painted c.1845. Friends who visited Dadd at this time commented on the wonderful work he was producing, with bizarre inscriptions in mingled French and English on the back. Dadd had also written to friends during the time he was travelling in the Middle East, and had described the experience of camping by the Dead Sea while crossing the desert on the way to visit a monastery.

Peter had not been sure enough of the painting's provenance to value it at the *Roadshow*, but it was bought by the British Museum in 1987 for £100,000. A number of other lost Dadds have subsequently come to light, and, since it is likely that he gave away a substantial amount of work while at Broadmoor, there may be many more waiting to be discovered.

Richard Dadd

Richard Dadd was born on 1 August 1817 in Chatham, Kent, the fourth of seven children. Educated at the King's School, Rochester, he began drawing at the age of 13, using the River Medway, the Royal Naval Dockyard and the landscape of Kent as inspiration. In 1837, Dadd began studying at the Royal Academy Schools and started to exhibit subjects taken from history and literature; he attracted great attention in 1841 with two small fairy paintings: *Titania Sleeping* and *Puck*. In 1842 he was commissioned to tour Europe and the Middle East with Sir Thomas Philips, the former mayor of Newport. It was during the tour that Dadd first showed signs of the madness that was to blight the rest of his life, and which led him, on his return from the tour, to murder his father. (Dadd believed that the Egyptian god Osiris controlled his will, a conviction that remained with him until he died.) He was committed first to Bethlem Hospital in London and then, in 1864, to Broadmoor in Berkshire. Dadd continued to paint throughout his incarceration, clinging to his identity as an artist. He died of consumption in January 1886.

George Richmond miniature

Found in St Helier, 1995; valued at £50–70,000. Sold at Bonhams in 1996 for £63,250.

Over the years Peter Nahum has been able to take the credit for spotting some of the finest paintings to be brought to the *Roadshow*. When this highly important miniature painted on ivory turned up during the visit to the island of Jersey, Peter placed on it the highest value, relative to surface area, of anything he had ever seen during his time on the programme.

It is always exciting to find something that has stayed in one family more or less since its creation, and this miniature, painted by the artist George Richmond, had come down from Richmond's daughter-in-law, who was the then owner's late husband's great-grandmother. It did go on the market in the 19th century, but, fortunately, was bought back by the artist's daughter Julia at a studio sale in Richmond-upon-Thames in 1897 for £210; it remained in the family from that point onwards. At one time the picture hung in the hallway of the family home, but eventually more modern images took its place, and the miniature was finally relegated to the attic.

George Richmond

Born in 1809, the young artist George Richmond studied at the Royal Academy Schools, where he formed a lifelong friendship with the celebrated artist Samuel Palmer. Together with Edward Calvert, another painter, the men joined a small group that worshipped the poet and artist William Blake, and was based in an artists' community in Shoreham, Kent. Calling themselves 'The Ancients', the members of the group followed a very simple, pastoral life, based on the romantic notion that ancient man was greatly superior to modern man. Following his marriage, and the need to support his growing family, Richmond started to paint portraits and became highly successful. He died in 1896 at the age of 86, having exhibited regularly at the Royal Academy for nearly six decades, between 1825 and 1884. His ideal of portraiture was, he said, 'the truth lovingly told'.

To Peter it was a very special painting. 'It comes', he maintained, 'from the most intensely visionary and romantic period in British art.' Entitled *In the First Garden*, the miniature measures a mere 21.6 x 14.6cm (8½ x 5¾in). Richmond painted it in 1828, at the age of 19, when he was staying with a group of fellow-artists and followers of the famed poet and artist William Blake in Shoreham, Kent.

In 1831 Richmond married Julia Tatham, the love of his life, and the couple went on to have 15 children, of whom 10 survived their infancy. The romantic idealism and simple way of life that Richmond followed at Shoreham produced the lyrical serenity possessed by pictures such as *In the First Garden*. It was an approach, however, that

unfortunately did not provide the regular income needed to support his large family. As a consequence the artist turned his hand to portrait painting and became one of its leading exponents. His portrait of Charlotte Brontë hangs today in the National Portrait Gallery in London.

Before coming to the *Roadshow* the owner thought that the painting might be worth approximately £3,000, and did not even have it insured separately from her other household items. She told her two children that she would split the value with them, whatever it happened to be. 'I wish my husband were still alive to share this with us,' she said, when Peter revealed to her the astonishing value of the family heirloom.

97

Henrietta Ronner painting

Found in Inverness, 1994; valued at £15–20,000. Current value up to £30,000.

Some valuable boot-sale bargains have been brought to *Roadshows* over the past few years, but this painting by Dutch artist Henrietta Ronner beat them all. Bought for just 50p, it had been stored in the owner's garden shed.

With no idea of its value, the owner's sister asked her to take it along when she heard that the *Roadshow* was coming to town. Unfortunately, during the car journey to the venue the painting became badly scratched. You can see the damage at the bottom left of the crimson-covered armchair on which the little terrier is sitting. A red-faced sister received a gentle ticking off from Peter Nahum when she confessed how the damage had come about.

She soon found out why he thought the painting should have been treated with greater care. Her sister's bargain turned out to be worth many thousands of pounds, because Henrietta Ronner was a leading

19th-century Dutch artist. For 15 years she concentrated exclusively on depicting dogs; subsequently, however, she turned to cats, and it is these paintings that are sold for the most money today. As well as painting her own animals, Ronner made portraits of pets brought to her by doting owners. In order to capture her subjects' movements she devised a glass box in which the animals were placed amid various cushions and toys.

'[Ronner] has a proven track record, and prices have gone up considerably recently,' said Peter Nahum. 'In fact, the value of the paintings is dependent on the number of cats in any one study.' Given our obsession with animals, it is hardly surprising that her paintings find such a ready market today. The major auction houses hold regular sales devoted to animal subjects, and the works of artists such as Ronner are always at a premium – bought for 50p, this one sold at auction in the mid-1990s for £22,000.

Henrietta Ronner

Born Henrietta Knip in 1821, Ronner had parents, a grandfather and an aunt who were all eminent artists. Not surprisingly, she began to draw as a child, preferring to make studies of animals rather than of people. When she was 12 her father, by then blind, began to teach her. Ronner's obvious talent led to her first work being exhibited at the age of 16, and before long she was considered an established artist. She married in 1860 and settled in Brussels. By 1870, when Ronner began to study and paint cats rather than dogs, she had acquired a formidable reputation as an artist. She exhibited her work all over the world and was elected to numerous European academies. She won a large number of prizes and was also awarded the Cross of the Order of Leopold by the King of the Belgians. In her eighties she still painted for several hours every day. Henrietta Ronner died in 1909.

Glasgow Boys painting

Found in Motherwell, 1993; valued at £30–40,000.

The experts expect, and look forward to seeing, examples of work from the area where a *Roadshow* takes place. At Motherwell, however, Henry Wyndham was taken aback when presented with a collection of paintings by members of the Glasgow School, especially when the owner told him that there were more at home. His surprise turned to astonishment when he was told that this example of the work of Edward Atkinson Hornel, dated 1912, was bought by the owner's grandfather for £75.

By 1912 Hornel had become well known for his scenes of little girls, often against sandy bays, as here, or in other landscape settings. Hornel is a very popular Scottish painter, and many devotees of Scottish art consider their collections incomplete unless they contain at least one of his paintings.

Hornel was born in Victoria, Australia, in 1864, of Scottish parents who returned to their native country when he was two.

The family settled in Kirkcudbright, which was the inspiration for so much of Hornel's work. He studied at the Trustees Academy in Edinburgh and at the Academy in Antwerp. It was the work he undertook in Belgium that established him as a landscape painter.

Hornel met the artist George Henry in 1885. They shared a studio in Glasgow and worked together in Kirkcudbright for several years before visiting Japan in 1893–4. This trip had a profound effect on Hornel's work, and his Japanese paintings are considered by critics to be the best of all his output.

Hornel's low-key palette, seen in this picture, with its pattern of colours detracting from any particular emphasis on the subject, became the hallmark of his style. Although many of his later paintings of little girls (both European and oriental) are felt to be rather coy and mannered, it is also acknowledged that his use of colour lifted them well above the mundane.

Glasgow Boys

The name 'Glasgow Boys' was given to a loose-knit group of artists, of which Hornel (1864–1933) was a member, working in and around the Scottish city at the end of the 19th century; they are also known as the Glasgow School. They worked in many styles and media, but were united by a hostility towards both the Royal Scottish Academy in Edinburgh, and what they judged to be its intense parochialism, and the picturesque romanticism of their elders, whom they referred to as 'The Gluepots' because of their use of a heavy brown varnish. The Glasgow Boys worked in various parts of Scotland during the warm months, generally returning to their studios in the city in the winter. By the end of the 19th century they had dispersed, but they are considered to have rejuvenated Scottish art and had a profound influence in Europe, particularly on the Secessionist Movement in Vienna.

Foujita painting

Found in Islington, London, 1990; valued at £50,000. Current value may be less, as a result of the fluctuating situation in the Far East.

The American gentleman who brought in this early example of the work of the Japanese artist Tsuguharu Foujita was sitting drinking a cup of coffee outside a café and watching the queue move slowly into the building across the road where the *Roadshow* was taking place.

His wife suggested that when the queue grew a little shorter they should go home (which was, fortuitously, just around the corner) and collect a painting that they had hanging on the wall. When they returned with their painting, Philip Hook thanked them very much for bringing him one of the most interesting and important items he had ever seen on the *Roadshow*.

He explained that Foujita was the most significant Japanese painter working in a western style this century, and pointed out his signature in both western and Japanese script. The painting of nudes was done in pen, ink and watercolour around 1920, when Foujita was establishing himself as an important member of the Paris School

that flourished between the two world wars. Paris was at the forefront of artistic development, and the work of the many artists based in the city during this period laid the foundations of much of our contemporary visual arts.

Many of these artists came from other countries, as, of course, did Foujita. If he frequented the salons and pavement cafés of the Left Bank, he would have been able to fraternise with other artists who are now internationally recognised, such as Chagall from Russia, Modigliani from Italy, Pascin from Bulgaria and Soutine from Lithuania. The Paris School is the name now given to all of the foreign artists who settled in Paris

at the beginning of the 20th century. At the time the city had 130 galleries – compared with other capitals that had around 30 – showing the work of some 60,000 artists, one third of whom were foreign.

In 1990 Japanese collectors were clamouring to buy back Foujita's paintings. When Philip revealed the value of this example, the owner – who had insured the picture on his household contents policy – visibly reeled with shock. He then turned to the woman behind him, quipping: 'Want to marry me now?' If he were to offer it for sale today, however, he might well discover that its value has fallen due to the current economic instability in the Far East.

Tsuguharu Foujita

Tsuguharu Foujita (1886–1968) was born in Tokyo into a Samurai family. After studying at that city's Imperial Academy of Fine Art between 1906 and 1910, travelling in China and visiting London, he settled in Paris in 1913. Apart from a world tour in 1929 and the years of the Second World War, which he sat out in Tokyo, he would spend the remainder of his life in Paris. Foujita started out by producing Parisian landscapes, and subsequently became known for his combination of still-life and nude studies. By 1925 he had developed his personal style, which the critics describe as a delicately mannered Expressionism that combines both Japanese and Western traits; it is a style very much in evidence in the picture shown here. In 1959 Foujita converted to Roman Catholicism; he also changed his first name to Leonard, in memory of Leonardo da Vinci.

Ming vases

Found at Waddesdon Manor, 1996; valued at £7–10,000 each. Current value the same.

The story of how two important Ming vases came to appear together on the *Roadshow* is one that Lars Tharp loves to recount. 'It was a happy accident,' he said. 'I spotted a lady standing in the queue and saw the covered Ming vase bulging out of her basket. I didn't need to see very much of it to know that it would be worth recording for the programme, so we booked her into the schedule. About an hour and a half later I saw another lady with the uncovered jar, also Ming, and thought it would be interesting and fun to record them together.'

The earlier, uncovered jar, dating from c.1530–50, was made in the shape of a wine jar, although it would probably only have been used as a decorative piece. In addition it would originally have been fitted with a cover. 'It is decorated with a central zone of bamboo, pine and prunus, which is known in Chinese iconography

as the "three friends of winter",' said Lars. 'Above it is a frieze of lotus flowers and below it lotus lappets, or stylized lotus flowers.' The owner had been given the vase by her mother, who had retrieved it from a friend's garage 30 years earlier. Since that time it had been used as a plant pot, either sitting by the fire or outside on the patio in all weathers – much to the owner's horror when she learned its value.

It would have been made for use in China, whereas the later, covered vase, was made around 1600 for export. This vase is painted with a classic lotus scroll, and its cover with panels depicting seated Chinese gentlemen. 'The vase is decorated very much in Dutch delft style,' said Lars, 'and would have been intended to appeal to the wealthy Europeans who were clamouring for oriental porcelain around this time. To own an impressive collection tremendously enhanced one's social standing.'

Ming dynasty porcelain

The Ming dynasty spanned the years 1369–1644. Many emperors reigned within this lengthy period, during which the quality and variety of the porcelain varied a great deal. Ming means 'brilliant', and it was during this era that the potters working at Jingdezhen perfected the techniques of decorating in underglaze and onglaze enamels to create beautifully balanced pieces. 'They are often the sort of pieces that go unrecognized,' explained Lars. 'Two examples include a 16th-century bowl worth £4–7,000 that had been used for the dog's water, and a 15th-century bowl decorated with geraniums that had stored the washing-up brushes and was sold for £240,000.' Late Ming export wares suffered from being hurriedly produced and decorated to satisfy the huge demand from Europe.

Dwight stoneware plaque

Found in Walsall, 1997. This rare piece remains of highly speculative value.

One of the most reassuring aspects of the *Roadshow* is the generosity that exists between the experts, who always seek the advice of a colleague if faced by a mystery. At Walsall, in 1997, this strange weather-beaten plaque turned up in front of Victoria Leatham. She took it to Gordon Lang, senior tutor in Works of Art courses at Sotheby's Institute and a long-serving member of the *Roadshow* team.

Gordon took a deep breath when he saw it. As he looked at the deeply carved features and the curling hair/foliage around the face, the objects that sprang to mind were a rare London delft figure of Apollo, which had been sold at Sotheby's in 1986 for £54,000, and the bust of Charles II by John Dwight c.1673 at the Victoria and Albert Museum. The style of the plaque convinced him that it was 17th-century salt-glazed stoneware, a very hard material, which had survived for over 300 years.

The owner had grown up with the plaque, which had been found on the beach near the family holiday cottage on the Welsh coast in the 1960s. The piece was given the name 'Stoneface' and left outside in all weathers. Eventually it was taken indoors and lived at the back of the fireplace. After the *Roadshow*, Gordon began to pursue some intensive research on a piece that was obviously rare and interesting enough to be of museum quality.

Finally staff at the Museum of London produced some fragments of pottery made in Fulham, west London, that looked very similar and tied the plaque more tightly to the name of John Dwight. With something as old and speculative as Stoneface an element of mystery will always remain, but Gordon is now as sure as he can be that it was produced at Dwight's workshop. The greater conundrum is how it managed to wash up on the Welsh shoreline.

John Dwight

John Dwight (c.1633–1703) was a pioneer in the development of English pottery, despite the fact that he didn't take it up until he was nearly 40. He was the son of an Oxford gentleman of the same name and, after emerging from Christ Church, Oxford, in 1661, went on to become chaplain and registrar to four successive bishops of Chester between 1661 and 1670. He began experiments in pottery using clays he that he found in the Kennel pits at Haigh, near Wigan, Lancashire. In 1671 Dwight was granted a patent (which he would defend with legal actions against other potters, who were sometimes also former employees) for making 'Transparent earthenware commonly called porcellane or china …' and, it is thought, probably moved to Fulham in the same year. His salt-glazed stoneware figures are considered to be among the best English sculpture of the late 17th century.

Ozzy the Owl

Found in Northampton, 1989; valued at over £20,000. Sold at Phillips to The Potteries Museum and Art Gallery, Stoke-on-Trent, in 1990 for £22,000. Current value £30–40,000.

Occasionally a *Roadshow* discovery causes such a stir that it hits the headlines. So it was with 'Ozzy the Owl', a Staffordshire slipware drinking pot c.1685–1690 whose rarity and charm captured the hearts of the nation. As the owner unwrapped the layers of newspaper surrounding the piece, Henry Sandon knew exactly what he was looking at.

'Staffordshire slipware is one of the earliest identifiable types of pottery made in the area, and its production had more or less ceased by the beginning of the 18th century,' he said. 'Surviving pieces are very desirable, but this little drinking pot – the body would have been used as the jug and the separate head as the cup – was in feathered slipware, which is even rarer. An ordinary mug would have been an exciting find, but the figures, like Ozzy, are rarer still, so he really was a very important discovery.' The owl had been in the owner's family for many years and was used, with the cover removed, as a flower vase.

About ten owls have turned up in total, according to Henry – probably all made by the same person. He thinks that the maker simply loved owls and produced these cups as amusing little objects. They were made in rather a soft earthenware covered with a lead glaze, and were never meant to last for a long time. The decoration was made by putting coloured slip (liquid clay) onto the body of the pot and then feathering it with a quill before firing. The pieces were then dipped into a lead glaze and fired again.

Ozzy's owner had travelled by bus to the *Roadshow*, but so immediate was the interest surrounding the discovery that the BBC sent her home in a taxi accompanied by two policemen, much to her mother's consternation when she opened the door.

After the piece was sold the owner told Henry that she had used the money to adopt five orphans from around the world. Ozzy now lives in a custom-built cabinet in the Stoke-on-Trent City Museum – a special home for a very important owl.

Staffordshire slipware

The type of feathering with which Ozzy the Owl is decorated appears to be unique to Staffordshire, although other types of slipware were made elsewhere in England, particularly at Wrotham in Kent between c.1612 and 1710. The Staffordshire potters were making pieces for ordinary domestic purposes for the people who lived in the area. They used a red or buff-coloured clay – which was not of the best quality – for the work, and decorated the pieces in brown and cream slip (liquid clay). This was applied in one of three ways: it could be trailed onto the surface, or dotted on, or simply poured onto the object. While still wet the slip was scratched through with a special tool, in the technique known as *sgraffito*, to create the pattern. Only a few signed pieces of this work have survived up to the present day, and the majority of early slipware is unmarked.

Lowestoft porcelain teapot

Found in Chepstow, 1996; valued at £3,000. Sold at Phillips in 1996 for £4,370.

A piece of Lowestoft worth between £400 and £500 – very nice, thought Chris Spencer, as a customer placed this teapot on his table with the undated side towards him. When Chris turned it around, however, and saw the inscription it bore – 'John & Eliz. Gibbs' as well as a date, '1770' – he was less understated.

As a leading authority on Lowestoft porcelain, Chris knew from the inscription that he was looking at a very rare survivor of a service manufactured by the factory to commemorate the wedding of 'John & Eliz. Gibbs'. Only one other item bearing the same inscription, also a piece of teaware, is known to exist today.

The teapot, which was given to the mother of the lady who brought it to the *Roadshow* by her employer in Essex, had travelled to Australia and back unscathed. Not greatly loved by the family, it was about to be sold or even given away on the other side of the world. When the owner telephoned her family to let them know of her intentions, however, they persuaded her to bring it on a visit to England because they knew the *Roadshow* was coming to town. And the teapot's reprieve turned out to be a cause of celebration for the family.

Many of the pieces produced by the Lowestoft factory, such as this teapot, were decorated in underglaze blue, both painted and transfer-printed. The very best pieces, which were manufactured around 1760, are comparable to Worcester porcelain, and some carry a crescent mark similar to that used at Worcester. Later pieces have more in common with those produced at the company's factory in Bow, in the East End of London, and in fact a number of Bow workers moved to take up employment at Lowestoft. Collectors love the naïvety of the pieces, and are prepared to pay high prices for the most desirable items. For instance, a small circular birth tablet, only 8cm (3in) in diameter and inscribed 'Thos. Anderson Born Sept. 13th, 1790', made £5,290 at Phillips, again in 1996.

The Lowestoft factory

The Lowestoft factory is renowned for inscribed and dated pieces such as the teapot shown here, which was made as a commemorative piece for a wedding. About 400 of these items are known, says Chris Spencer, which allows all the other wares to be grouped and dated because both the paste formula and the style of decoration that was used underwent changes over the years. The successful enterprise at Lowestoft was initiated by a group of East Anglian businessmen: notably Philip Walker (who was a farmer), Robert Browne (who was a blacksmith) and Obed Aldred (a bricklayer who owned his own kiln). Once a good, workable soft-paste porcelain formula had been found, the men were able to go into production with their new venture. The factory continued in production from 1756 right up until its closure in 1799, after which the proprietors continued to sell the wares that they had made well into the 19th century.

Mrs Ambrose's punch pot

Found in Liverpool, 1988; valued at £5–6,000. Current value £14–18,000.

ittle did Mrs Ambrose know just how drastically her life was about to change as she stood in the long queue that formed from early morning when the *Roadshow* visited Liverpool in 1988. Wrapped safely in her bag was the now-famous piece her mother had always used as the family teapot. Mrs Ambrose cherished it for sentimental reasons and kept it wrapped in a tea towel on top of the wardrobe in her bedroom. In fact, she was a rather reluctant visitor to the event. Her sister had persuaded her to come, but she had nothing to bring, she said, except her mother's teapot, and because it was cracked and chipped she thought that she might not be allowed in.

She turned out to be one of the great stars of the *Roadshow*, for her teapot, a Whieldon-type punch pot, c.1745–50, was an important find. Revealing its true value to Mrs Ambrose in front of the cameras

was the best part of the day for David Battie, who delighted in quoting steadily increasing amounts to the startled owner.

'I asked her what she'd think if I told her it might be worth £150, building up until we got to £2,000. She said, "You're joking. I know you!" I finally quoted £5–6,000. It was the perfect combination of delightful customer and wonderful object.' The pot went up for sale at Sotheby's with a reserve price of £5,000 and was sold for £14,300. Mrs Ambrose bought the council house she had lived in for so many years and became a regular visitor to the *Roadshow* whenever it came to the north of England.

Made in creamware with the spout modelled as a snake, and decorated with mottled green, yellow and brown lead glazes, Mrs Ambrose's punch pot belongs to a range of pottery known as Whieldon-type wares. It was produced during the mid-18th century in Staffordshire.

Whieldon-type wares

Thomas Whieldon (1719–95), Josiah Wedgwood's partner from 1754 to 1759, was one of the century's most important potters working in the Staffordshire area and the first to develop mottled glazes, which also include tortoiseshell and agateware. The powder colours were dusted onto the pieces before firing; they then mingled to create the effect. Many other small potteries produced similar wares so, unless pieces can be proved to have been made by Whieldon, they are called Whieldon-type wares. In the mid-18th century, when this pot was made, punch drinking was a popular male pastime. The drink was brandy or rum mixed with orange and lemon juice, and spices. Punch bowls in silver, Chinese porcelain or delft were used for cold punch, but a warming mixture was served from a punch pot like this, which resembles a giant teapot but without the strainer at the base of the spout.

Porcelain snuffbox

Found in Horsham, 1996; valued at £6–7,000. Current value the same.

Only 5.75cm (2¼in) long, this German porcelain snuffbox, gold-mounted and painted with hunting scenes, was a little gem, and David Battie tackled it with great enthusiasm. The owner had inherited the box from her grandmother and had been told that it was Battersea enamel. In fact, not only was it not enamel, David was able to tell her, but it wasn't English either. It was probably made by the celebrated Berlin factory around 1760, but the style of decoration owed a great deal to Meissen, the first and most influential porcelain factory in Europe.

It is very unusual, David explained, to come across a really good Continental porcelain snuffbox. They are not usually so finely painted or in such good condition, and he had seen only about half a dozen in the past 20 years that compared favourably with this example. There remained a slight question mark over its origins, however,

because porcelain decorators moved around. For instance, two of the best-known Berlin factory painters, Karl Wilhelm Böhme and Johann Balthasar Borrmann, both came from Meissen, as did Friedrich Elias Meyer, the *Modellmeister* (chief modeller). However, the paste always varies slightly, which aids identification, and this looked very much like a Berlin piece.

At this time, around 1765, snuff taking was an important social ritual, and much was made of the act itself. Although the habit became ingrained across the social classes, the owner of this piece would have been a wealthy gentleman, probably with a collection of several fine snuffboxes. As he left his house to meet his friends he would select one to slip into his pocket. Normally the boxes are worn on the base from being pushed about on tables, but this example is in pristine condition – a very important factor in the assessment of its value.

The Berlin factory

There were actually two Berlin porcelain factories. The first, founded in 1752 by a merchant granted a monopoly by Frederick the Great, was forced to close after five years. The second, built in the Leipzigerstrasse by Johann Ernst Gotzkowsky in 1761, was purchased by Frederick the Great in 1763 and became a royal factory. Frederick gave the factory special privileges; he also prohibited the sale of Meissen in the Prussian territories to ensure commercial security. The factory continued to flourish throughout the 18th century, although the pieces made during its first decade – such as this snuffbox – are the finest, with designs inspired by the paintings of artists such as Watteau and Boucher. In 1819 an elaborate service, painted with scenes from his battles, was presented to the Duke of Wellington; it can now be seen in his former home, Apsley House, in London.

Davenport plates

Found at Wellington, 1994; valued at £1,500–2,000. Current value £2,500–3,000.

Every *Roadshow* expert, whatever his or her speciality and area of expertise, has a favourite factory, maker or period. Terence Lockett's choice would be the Staffordshire factory of Davenport. He has, in fact, written two books on the factory and its work; the first was published in 1972, and the other, which was written together with Geoffrey Godden, appeared in 1990. Terence was therefore delighted when a colleague called him over during a *Roadshow* to show him eight finely painted and gilded Davenport plates by Richard Ablott; all of them had been decorated with scenes of Scottish lochs.

The owner of the plates, a young lady, had inherited them from her grandmother, who in turn had bought them in a junk shop in Scotland in the 1950s for about £20. Each plate was stamped with '1920' on the base, and the owner of the shop

had simply assumed that they were fakes that had been produced during that year. The present owner's grandmother had no reason to suppose anything different, and as a result had been completely unaware of their true worth. It turned out, however, that '1920' was in fact the pattern number, rather than the date; the plates had, in fact, been produced in 1865 and, moreover, were undoubtedly genuine, which made them a very exciting and unexpected find for Terence Lockett.

'Not only were they superbly painted and in excellent condition,' commented Terence, 'but each one of the plates had been signed. Ablott was one of the few artists working at Davenport who signed his pieces. He was born in Canada, the son of an English soldier who served in Manitoba, and subsequently came back to England as a young man. He worked

initially at the Derby factory and then at Coalport, before moving in 1860 to Davenport, where he remained until 1896. Ablott specialized in portraying landscapes such as these and would have turned to books for inspiration rather than making a trip up to Scotland to observe the scenery.'

Terence turned his attentions to Davenport after Rockingham (on which he also wrote a book 30 years ago) became too expensive to collect. 'It was during the mid-1960s that my late wife and I decided we'd like to collect something that was still affordable and available', he explained. 'We searched through all the standard reference books and decided on Davenport – and the books followed. In all my years of collecting and researching their wares I've only ever seen one collection of plates that would be comparable to this, but those were unsigned and not as well painted.'

The Davenport factory

The period of the Davenport factory's existence (1794–1887) spanned the majority of the 19th century, which was a fascinating period in the history of the Potteries. The factory was founded in Longport, Staffordshire, by John Davenport, a merchant who provided the initial money for the enterprise to get off the ground. The business would remain in the hands of the same family until it later began to go downhill and eventually closed in 1887. In the early years the owners of the factory had started out by manufacturing blue transfer-printed earthenware, but after 1820 they went on to produce porcelain. Tea services and dessert services were the staple product made by Davenport by this time, and, like Rockingham, the factory manufactured a dessert service for King William IV. Many of the Davenport wares imitated Derby wares. Richard Ablott – the maker of the plates that are shown here – was not the only decorator to have worked at the Derby factory, as the renowned artists Thomas Steele and James Rouse had both also been there before making their marks at Davenport.

Beilby toastmaster's glass

Found at Newcastle Emlyn, 1994; valued at £7–8,000. Current value up to £9,000.

It was a quiet start to the day, so John Sandon decided to walk along the queue asking the patiently waiting members of the public whether they had anything interesting hidden away in their boxes and baskets. One gentleman replied that, yes, he had some nice glasses with him, and from the safety of its copious wrappings he produced this stunning Beilby toastmaster's glass, which was made between 1765 and 1770. The man was immediately ushered away to join the day's recording schedule, and later, in front of the cameras, John was able to tell him in detail just how significant his piece really was.

The value of the glass increased with each point of interest that was discovered. First of all, the white enamelling, and particularly the care and delicacy with which the decoration had been undertaken, suggested to John that William Beilby was the maker. Beilby and his sister Mary were the foremost glass enamellers working in the late 18th century, making this piece a valuable and important find. Second, on the other side of the glass is inscribed the word 'Temperance', which refers to one of the friendly societies allied to the Masonic movement and based in Newcastle-upon-Tyne in the north of England. John knew that the Beilby family worked in Newcastle, and this additional detail strengthened the case for attributing the glass to them. The connection with the Masonic movement also added to its commercial value.

Lastly, the fact that this is a toastmaster's glass, with a heavy foot and thick stem that were designed to withstand being banged down on the table after each toast, further increased the interest of the piece. The bowl, too, is particularly thick. The reason for this being that the glass could then contain only a small quantity of liquid, which would have allowed the toastmaster to preserve his equilibrium while all about him were losing theirs. All in all, the glass proved to be a fascinating find.

Beilby glass

Enamelling on glass became more widespread in Britain after 1760, and the Beilby family was one of its main exponents. William, the fourth of seven children, was apprenticed to a maker of enamel pieces (snuffboxes and so on) in Bilston, in the West Midlands, one of the main centres of this work in the 18th century. After his father's business failed the family moved to Newcastle, where William established a successful business painting with white enamel on clear glass, a technique that he had begun to use earlier. His sister Mary joined him, and their work soon became widely admired. William painted in both white and coloured enamels, but examples of the latter are much rarer. Flowers, fruiting vines, hops and barley were favourite subjects, as were detailed scenes of classical ruins, landscapes and sporting events. William also produced important coloured armorial and commemorative pieces. The very best examples have fetched £50–60,000 at auction.

Renaissance gold plaque

Found in Farnham, 1991; valued at £30–50,000. Would be classed as priceless today.

Simon Bull is not only an authority on clocks, watches and scientific instruments, but also a connoisseur of Renaissance works of art. So it was fortunate that he was on the team when this extraordinarily rare and beautiful gold plaque, made between 1570 and 1580, was brought to the *Roadshow*. The owner inherited it from her father, who had been a collector of such pieces.

'He bought it at Christie's at a time when this kind of thing interested people,' said Simon. 'Currently, for some reason, 14th-, 15th- and 16th-century European works of art are not fashionable.' It is his contention that any area of the decorative arts that requires scholarship in order to be properly understood is in the doldrums. Luckily for the owner, Simon recognized at once the importance of the plaque, one of a group of six reputed to have been mounted originally in an Italian cabinet owned by the Borghese family, one of the wealthiest and most powerful of the time.

Similar plaques are kept in a major museum in Berlin. Originally they were thought to be the work of Benvenuto Cellini, considered by many to be one of the greatest goldsmiths of his age. However, further research has suggested that they were made by another celebrated goldsmith of the period, De la Portas.

The plaque, with its four corners set with cornelians, a red variety of chalcedony, shows Atalanta and fellow-hunters killing a boar. In the Greek legend, Atalanta, a swift and fearless huntress skilled with bow and spear, joined in the quest to kill the savage boar that had laid waste the lands of King Oineus – his punishment for failing to make a sacrifice to Artemis as thanks for a fruitful year. The monstrous beast made short work of most of the men, but Atalanta's arrow flew with an aim straight and true. The boar fell, and Atalanta was presented with its head as a trophy. One of the great legends, this story is often depicted in painting and works of art of the Renaissance.

Renaissance works of art

The Italian Renaissance, a period when all the arts flourished, began in the late 14th century and so had been growing and gathering strength by the time the cabinet onto which this plaque was mounted was made. Powerful dynasties such as the Medici and Borghese families patronized great artists and craftsmen of the day, allowing them to recreate the best examples of Classical architecture and works of art in media from mural decoration and furniture to metalwork, pottery and jewellery. Cabinets were often made from ebony by makers working in Augsburg, Germany. The wood was so highly prized that it was hallmarked, and the finished piece was often mounted with carved stone panels set into the drawer and cupboard fronts. By the time that this plaque was made, furniture had grown more elaborate. With every one of these exquisite gold plaques intact, the original cabinet must have been a remarkable sight.

Boxed tea caddies

Found in Yeovilton, 1991; valued at £15,000. Current value the same.

Ian Pickford is no stranger to top-quality English silver. Even so, this boxed set, comprising a pair of tea caddies and a matching sugar bowl, all with wonderful chased decoration, in immaculate condition and still in the original shagreen-covered case, was quite out of the ordinary. 'They were a fairly standard shape and design for the maker, Samuel Taylor, and these things are not rare, but the provenance made them very valuable,' said Ian.

The owner also brought an oil painting of her ancestors done just before they were married; the caddies were made in 1750 as a wedding present. The family coat of arms was engraved on each piece. The unbroken line of descent, combined with the fact that one of the descendants had been Elizabeth Fry, made them exceptionally interesting.

Elizabeth Fry (1780–1845) was the famous Quaker prison reformer who also campaigned to improve conditions for the homeless in Brighton and London. She was born Elizabeth Gurney in Norwich and married Joseph Fry in 1800. In 1813 she visited London's Newgate Prison and was appalled by the sight of 300 women and their children living in terrible conditions. She devoted the rest of her life to prison reform, both in England and overseas, and to improving asylum conditions, despite her husband's bankruptcy in 1828.

The caddies have not come on the market, but pieces such as this, which have never done the rounds of auction houses and dealers, and which have such interesting histories, always command high prices when they are offered for sale. 'I would normally put a value of £5–6,000 on something like this, even in such excellent condition,' said Ian, 'so they are a splendid example of how much the history of an object can affect its value. Seeing them at the *Roadshow* made for a very interesting day.'

Samuel Taylor

The dates of the London silversmith responsible for these tea caddies are unknown, but he was apprenticed in 1737 to John Newton and became a Freeman of the Worshipful Company of Goldsmiths in 1744 and a Liveryman in May 1751. He entered his first mark as a 'large worker' in 1744 and his second in 1757. Silversmiths tended to be classified as 'large' or 'small' workers, depending on the pieces they made. Objects such as salt cellars, salvers and tankards were produced by large workers, and little boxes, buckles, buttons and so on by small workers. Taylor probably took over Newton's business and appears to have specialized in tea caddies and sugar bowls – his mark is rarely seen on anything else. The caddies were for green and black tea. At one time it was thought that the central bowl was for blending the two, but it has now been proved that such pieces were always meant for sugar.

Paul Storr salt cellars

Found in Salisbury, 1990; valued at £40,000. Current value £65–70,000.

Penny Brittain remembers the day on which the Paul Storr salt cellars arrived at Salisbury Cathedral as the most nail-biting in the many years she has been involved with the *Roadshow*. 'I was working on reception and the gentleman turned up with one of them in a brown paper bag. He asked me if I thought it might be brass and wanted to know what it was for. By the time he had it out of the bag I had seen the maker's mark for Paul Storr. I asked him if he had any more, and when he told me there were three others I begged him to go back and get them. He was very reluctant, so we put him in a taxi and waited.'

The owner did not turn up again until Evensong, by which time Penny had almost given up hope. 'He arrived at last with his wife and the other pieces. His father and mother had been in service and were given the salts as a retirement present. He had kept them in a plastic bag at the bottom of a bedroom cupboard for the six years since his father had given them to him.' Brand Inglis recorded them as the last item of the day – one of the most memorable in his years as a silver expert on the *Roadshow*. 'They were the most beautiful sculptural objects and made by one of our greatest ever silversmiths and goldsmiths,' he said.

The four silver-gilt salts were modelled as shells held aloft by mermaids or mermen; three were made in 1813 and one in 1811. Brand explained that Paul Storr had probably been inspired by a similar design (kept at Windsor Castle in Berkshire) by Nicholas Sprimont – the celebrated 18th-century silversmith who went on to found the Chelsea porcelain factory. Storr worked for Rundell, Bridge & Rundell, who made many pieces for the wealthiest patrons, including the royal family, and he would therefore have seen many of the treasures in the Royal Collection.

After the owner had recovered from the shock of Brand's valuation of £40,000, he went home a happy man. 'If my daughter-in-law hadn't told me the *Roadshow* was coming to Salisbury,' he said, 'the salts would still be sitting in the bottom of that cupboard, and if anything had happened to my wife and I, the children would have had no idea of their value. They would probably have gone in a job-lot house clearance.'

Later bought at auction by the Salters' Company for £66,000, the cellars are now at Salters' Hall in the City of London.

Paul Storr

The craftsman Paul Storr (1771–1844), who created the beautiful salt cellars shown here, is generally considered to be the most important of the Regency silversmiths. He was at his most active, in terms of production, between 1797 and 1821. Storr first registered his mark at Goldsmiths' Hall, London, in 1792, and shortly afterwards he joined the renowned firm of Rundell & Bridge, later becoming a partner in the company. By 1805 the firm had become Rundell, Bridge & Rundell. Its craftsmen were goldsmiths to many important, wealthy and influential clients, whose number included George III and his consort Charlotte Sophia. The company also produced some significant pieces for the Prince Regent. Paul Storr designed and made many of these items. He left the company in 1821 and went into partnership with John Mortimer, before finally retiring in 1839.

Crawley silver

Found in Crawley, 1993; valued at over £200,000. Part of the collection was subsequently sold at auction in 1994 for £78,000.

Every *Roadshow* expert begins the day hoping to see at least one really wonderful object before the queues start to disappear, but as Ian Pickford took his seat at Crawley in West Sussex he could hardly have predicted the treat that was in store for him that day.

A young man and his mother sat down at his table and began pulling piece after piece of fine English silver out of carrier bags. 'It was the very best collection of silver I have ever seen on the *Roadshow*', said Ian afterwards. The pieces simply kept on coming, until he eventually valued the total haul at over £200,000. The owner's late husband had developed a genuine passion for silver, and had accumulated the collection throughout the 1960s and 1970s. His widow had no idea of the full extent of the collection until, after her husband's death, she started to discover pieces that had been carefully stored in different parts of the house, together with all the receipts from when the purchases were made.

'The man had an unerring eye for the very best pieces,' said Ian, marvelling at the collection of tankards, which included a rare Commonwealth example of 1653 along with tankards made during the reigns

of Queen Anne, James II and William III. A rare three-compartment snuffbox was dated to 1740, while a vinaigrette from 1842 carried the mark of the renowned silversmith Nathaniel Mills. A small

The best of Crawley

Top right: James I wine bowl (1607). Sold in 1994 for £13,000, it was later sold at Christie's £28,750. It is believed to be the only James I example in existence.

Bottom right: stag's-head stirrup cup (1864). Bought in 1970 for £470, this stirrup cup sold in 1994 for just under £10,000 and would now be worth £15,000. A stirrup cup modelled on a stag's head, rather than a fox's head, is unusual and therefore highly desirable.

Opposite, top, left to right: Queen Anne tankard (1707) by Alice Sheene; sold in 1994 for £6,350, it would now be worth over £10,000. James II tankard (1688); sold in 1994 for £8,625, it would now fetch £10–12,000. William III tankard (1698) by William Andrew; sold in 1994 for £3,500, it would now be worth £6,500.

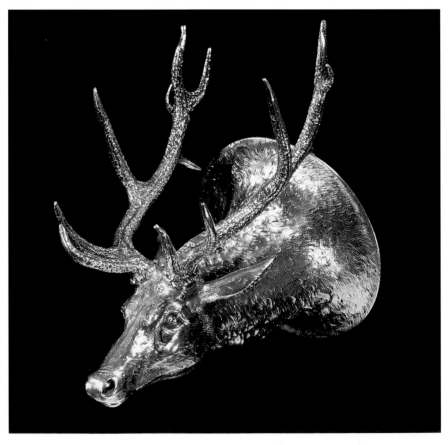

rectangular box, which is inlaid with a piece of the famous Boscobel oak in which the future Charles II sheltered, has been kept by the late owner's son.

'Full marks to your father,' was Ian's comment to the young man when the long recording of the pieces was finally complete. 'He was obviously a great connoisseur.' The son, reeling from the succession of high valuations placed on every piece, replied: 'Well, I'm glad you know what you're on about!'

Gold and coral teething rattle

Found in Rochdale, 1991; valued at £7–10,000. Current value £8–12,000.

Long before infant hygiene and safety reached today's standards, it was quite common for a baby in a well-to-do household to be given a silver teething rattle fitted with a tapering stick of red coral. Hung with bells that jingled merrily and kept the baby entertained, the stick was considered ideal chewing material for a teething infant. Many battered examples have been brought to the *Roadshow*, with squashed or missing bells and the stick either broken or covered in indentations made by tiny teeth – ample evidence that these items were considered perfectly acceptable playthings for babies.

Ian Harris was quite taken aback to see this exceptional example. Not only was it in 18-carat gold rather than silver, but also it was produced in London rather than Birmingham (where most were made), was in mint condition and, at 18cm (7in) long, was larger than most. It turned out that the owner's husband's aunt had given him the rattle when he was a baby. It was made in 1860 by Charles Rawlings and William Summers, two silversmiths who worked in partnership in London.

It may well have been commissioned by a wealthy client who had been asked to be godparent to a new baby and ordered it as a christening present. The parents clearly valued this very generous gift, because its condition tells us that the child was never allowed to play with it. In 1991, Ian valued the handle alone at £500.

Charles Rawlings and William Summers

Rawlings and Summers began a formidable partnership in 1829. Both sons of goldsmiths, they are well known for their high-quality pieces made in silver and gold, especially small items such as snuffboxes and babies' rattles. Rawlings was first apprenticed to one Edward Coleman, as a watch finisher, before entering his first mark as a silversmith in 1817. It was while he was working in Brook Street, Holborn (close to the City of London), that he teamed up with Summers. In 1839 they moved to Great Marlborough Street, in the heart of the West End, and worked together until 1863. Summers died in 1890, but Rawlings's demise has not been recorded. However, the wonderful objects that they produced live on today, appreciated by collectors everywhere.

Japanese bronze and silver elephant

Found in Queensferry, 1991; valued at £10–15,000. Current value £12–16,000.

If the closing years of the 19th century were characterized by opulent design, by a mishmash of styles and techniques, and by the flaunting of wealth created by the Industrial Revolution, then this Japanese bronze elephant with his silver cargo is the embodiment of all those elements. James Collingridge certainly found it a remarkable sight when it was put before him in 1991.

The owner's grandfather bought the elephant at a house sale in Liverpool at the beginning of the Second World War. There were no written records in the family, but it was thought that he paid around £30 for it. The piece was made during the Meiji Period (1868–1912), when Japan was exporting countless shiploads of decorative goods to the West after a long period of self-imposed isolation known as *sakoku* (closed country). Embroidered textiles, woodblock prints and pottery and porcelain flooded into countries on both sides of the Atlantic to satisfy a market hungry for exotic goods.

This piece is so extravagant that it may have been made to order for a wealthy customer. Such an owner would probably have delighted in displaying it prominently, so that acquaintances would have been left in no doubt as to his spending power. The object serves no useful purpose, but is a superb reminder of the exceptional skills of the craftsmen who created it. The saddle section under the howdah is cloisonné enamel, and the silver urn topped with an eagle is fitted with shibayama panels; both details are made to the highest standards.

After the Satsuma Rebellion of 1876–7 and the official end of Japan's ancient feudal system, an edict was published forbidding the samurai and other classes to wear the swords that, over the centuries, had been elevated to works of art. At the same time Japanese men began to abandon their traditional costumes in favour of Western dress, and no longer needed the skills of the ivory carvers to make the netsuke (toggles) and other accoutrements they wore with the kimono. An army of metalworkers and carvers suddenly found themselves having to adapt their skills to other forms to make a living. This elephant is a good example of their ingenuity.

Cloisonné and shibayama

The opulent piece shown here employs two intricate decorative techniques: cloisonné (for the elephant's saddle area) and shibayama (for the panels on the silver urn). Cloisonné is the term used to describe a method of decorating metal with enamel. The technique involves covering the base of an object (which might be made of copper, silver or gold) with a network of wires soldered to the surface in order to create a network of cloisons, or compartments. These compartments are then filled with an enamel paste, which is made from powdered glass mixed with coloured metallic-oxide pigments. Shibayama is the description used for a piece of ivory that has been inlaid with mother-of-pearl, coral, horn and stained ivory; this type of piece was often also enriched with gold lacquer.

Russian silver pendant

Found in Brussels, 1994; valued at £10–15,000. Current value the same.

It is not often that a piece of jewellery steeped in the romance and exoticism of foreign imperial powers turns up on the *Roadshow*. This glorious pendant, modelled as a capital 'A', was given to the owner's grandmother's great-great-aunt by Tsarina Maria Federovna, the penultimate Tsarina (1870–80) and wife of Tsar Alexander III. The aunt had been a lady-in-waiting at the Russian court in the late 19th century, and received the pendant on her retirement.

After she died, family quarrels led to the sale of the piece. Sadly, it seemed lost to the family until the owner's grandmother, travelling in Finland, found a picture and description of the piece in an auction catalogue in Helsinki and bought it back

for the sum of £2,000. Several of the rose-cut diamonds were missing, but these have now been replaced. The Tsarina's monogram is worked into the piece, which is topped with the Russian imperial crown. Unusually, it carries no Russian hallmarks.

Diamonds

Brilliant cutting evolved from the early 18th to the early 20th century, with the intention of reflecting as much light as possible through the top of the stone; to this end the 'table' (the flat surface at the top) became larger. The rose cut is a form of brilliant cut, but its standard 24 triangular facets on the top rise to a shallow, pointed peak.

Mughal gold bracelets

Found in Peebles, 1995; valued at £10–15,000. Current value the same.

These brilliantly coloured, enamelled and jewel-encrusted Indian bracelets, known as *kadas*, were not at all what expert John Benjamin expected to see in Peebles. The owner's great-grandparents had spent much of their working lives in India; her great-grandfather was a civil engineer, and the bracelets had been given to her great-grandmother by a Mughal

prince. Normally part of a bride's dowry, bracelets of this kind would have been worn around the ankle or the upper arm.

The bracelets, both measuring 8cm (3in) in diameter, are modelled as confronting serpents, each with a lashing ruby tongue.

They were probably made around the middle of the 19th century from high-quality 22-carat gold, richly enamelled in royal and sky blue. After being decorated with patterns of flowers and birds, they were studded with table-cut diamonds.

The Mughal dynasty

Founded in 1526, the Mughal dynasty ended in 1858 on the death of Emperor Bahadur Shah. The jewellery made in this period was the definitive statement of the dynasty's wealth and influence. Emperors were literally weighed against an equivalent volume of jewels, and hundreds of workshops were kept busy making the objects, including hairpieces, bracelets like these, and belts and necklaces studded with precious stones.

Fabergé animals and brooch

Animals found on the Wirral, 1996; valued at £6–8,000 each.

Brooch found at Chatsworth, 1996; valued at £5,000.

Geoffrey Munn was rather shocked when the owner of these Fabergé animals, each only 8cm (3in) long, revealed that her children had played with them. However, he was less taken aback than she was when she heard their value.

Her story would probably have made Carl Fabergé smile. He loved children and, much to his customers' surprise, would often settle their children on the floor to play with his carvings. The Royal Collection at Sandringham, Norfolk, contains 500 of these hardstone animals. Fabergé was commissioned by Edward VII to produce these carvings, in various coloured stones, depicting many of the animals found at the royal residence at Sandringham. The pig is carved from rhodonite and the elephant from rock crystal, the hardest and rarest form of quartz and very difficult to work. Most of the stones Fabergé used came from the Urals and Siberia; among these were chalcedony, agate, obsidian and nephrite,

while for the eyes he used rose diamonds and cabochon rubies, and he sometimes modelled legs and tails in silver or gold.

Geoffrey often rummages through a family jewel box at the *Roadshow*. Far from risking missing the one good thing among the piles of baubles, he finds that anything of quality shouts out to him. The owner of the Fabergé heart-shaped enamelled brooch confessed that she was a jewellery addict. 'She bought mainly at auction,' said Geoffrey, 'and never paid more than £150

for anything. The brooch was in a bag ... She paid £30 for the lot, and when I told her what it was and how much it was worth she gasped and burst into tears.'

'It symbolizes luck in love,' Geoffrey continued. 'The diamond quatrefoil is for luck and the heart, of course, represents love. The four diamonds are worth only around £10 each. The value has nothing to do with the materials and everything to do with its being a wonderful piece of artistic jewellery from the workshops of Fabergé.'

Carl Fabergé

Carl Fabergé (1846–1920) was a man of few words but great vision. His family were natives of Picardy in northern France, Huguenots who fled the country in 1685 and settled in St Petersburg, changing their name twice to avoid discovery. Carl's father was a goldsmith, and the boy had a thorough training in the family business as well as serving an apprenticeship in Frankfurt. He travelled all over Europe, watching and learning, and by the age of 24 had taken control of the family business. After delivering one of his bejewelled Easter eggs to Tsar Alexander III in 1884 he was granted the Royal Warrant, and the prestige of his company was guaranteed. In 1900 he exhibited all the Imperial Eggs at the Exposition Internationale Universelle in Paris and was decorated with the Légion d'Honneur. When the Communists took over the House of Fabergé, after the 1917 Revolution, he fled to Switzerland and died there in exile in 1920.

William Burges silver-mounted bottle

Found in Skegness, 1996; valued at £30,000. Current value up to £50,000.

The most exciting discoveries are often the most unexpected. Paul Atterbury had left the table for a few moments when someone from Reception tapped him on the shoulder and showed him a small (around 18cm (7in) high) silver-mounted bottle. It was a moment of magic. The piece had arrived around 4pm, just as the doors were about to be closed, carefully wrapped and nestling in a shopping basket.

By looking at the style of decoration and the signature on the mount, Paul knew at once that it was a rare piece designed by the eccentric 19th-century English designer and architect William Burges. Moreover, it had been lost for over a hundred years.

Paul hurried back into the hall to share the find with fellow enthusiast David Battie, and together they talked to the owner in front of the cameras, revealing its history, while she filled them in on its whereabouts over the last 50 years. Her father bought the piece in 1949, in a junk shop off the Great North Road. She had treasured it for sentimental reasons, not realizing just how important it was.

The bottle itself (around which Burges designed) is 18th-century Chinese porcelain covered in a coffee glaze. The silver mounts are in the form of organic tendrils and trees encasing the body; a spider set with pearls sits on the cover. Burges's name and a date,

1864, are carried on an enamel band at the base. From the Tudor period onwards, elaborate mounts were added to pieces of porcelain (or even to coconuts and other objects considered rare and exotic).

By creating this piece, and many others of similar design, Burges, who worked in the Gothic Revival manner, was producing a treasury of pieces in his own inimitable version of this style.

Burges made a number of these objects for his own pleasure, keeping them at his house in Melbury Road in Kensington,

London. Much of his work, including this bottle, was photographed in the late 19th century, the album eventually finding its way into the Victoria and Albert Museum in London. By referring to the definitive book on Burges, Paul and David were able to match the photograph with the piece that stood in front of them.

In 1996, Paul and David valued it at £30,000, and in 1988 Sotheby's sold a jewelled and decorated Burges bottle for £40,000. Today, this example could be worth between £30,000 and £50,000.

William Burges

William Burges (1827–81) was a bizarre and eccentric figure, an architect and a designer working in the most elaborate Gothic Revival style, designing furniture, metalwork, jewellery and wallpapers. He was involved with the rebuilding and remodelling of the interiors of Cardiff Castle, in 1865, and Castell Coch, near Cardiff, ten years later, for his friend and client the Marquis of Bute. Burges's own house at 9 Melbury Road is considered a masterpiece, filled with colour and with ornate and intricately worked pieces that often incorporate painted panels, massive iron hinges and grotesquely carved birds and other animals.

Walnut longcase clock

Found in Bexhill-on-Sea, 1994; valued at £30,000. Current value £30–35,000.

When he saw this piece, Richard Price declared: 'This is probably one of the most unrestored, original and genuine walnut longcase clocks I have ever seen.' It was made during the first five years of the 18th century, some 40 years after the first longcase clocks were produced in any numbers. So many of these early clocks were altered according to later fashions that it is very pleasing to find one completely left alone for over 250 years.

Still in good working order, the clock had a beautiful matted centre (the brass in the centre of the dial has been hammered to give a frosted effect, more desirable than a plain brass centre) and superb rings around the winding holes. 'It also had a very slender seconds dial and lovely original spandrels that were very well cast,' said Richard. 'The overall proportions of the piece marked it out as really top-quality, and the case was in marvellous condition.'

The clock had an eight-day duration movement with a 28cm (11in) dial, and bore all the hallmarks of a top London maker. Indeed, Richard revealed that it came from the workshop of Joshua Wilson, a highly respected London clock maker. The case was in perfect proportion, with the slim trunk and long door. 'The walnut had turned a wonderful honey colour over 250 years, which added hugely to its desirability,' said Richard. The clock was sold soon afterwards to a private collector through a local dealer for around £25,000.

It is no wonder that Richard was so thrilled to find a longcase in such pristine condition. Clocks of this size formed part of the furnishings of a house, and no other area of antiques has been more the victim of 'improvement' than furniture. Arched tops were added to clocks later in the 18th century, and arched sections of brass were given to plain square dials. Pieces of wood were put under the movement to raise its height as the size of the case increased.

Other common alterations included removing a caddy-shaped top or cutting a plinth to make a clock shorter, and giving an early clock with a rising hood a hinged opening door so that it could be wound more easily in a room with a low ceiling.

18th-century English longcase clocks

We have several visionary men of the 17th century to thank for longcase clocks. The Dutch mathematical physicist and astronomer Christiaan Huygens invented the long pendulum in 1657; the technology was then taken up by a Dutch clock maker working in London, Ahasuerus Fromanteel, who began to make this new timekeeper. Other clock makers adopted the technique, and for several generations England led the field in this type of clockmaking. Robert Hooke and William Clement both helped to develop the anchor escapement c.1670. Earlier clocks were weight-driven, and had a verge escapement and a short pendulum. These were often inaccurate, but the long pendulum with an anchor escapement had a swing that took one second exactly and was maintained by its own momentum. It was probably the most significant invention in the history of timekeeping. Before long the idea arose of enclosing the pendulum in a case, to keep out dust, hide the workings and protect against accidental knocks.

Bracket clock

Found in Weymouth, 1995; valued at £10,000. Current value over £20,000.

Antique-clock expert Richard Price is always highly delighted when he comes across a good-quality bracket clock at a *Roadshow*. To his great satisfaction, the example shown here was not only beautifully made, but also very unusual – especially for a clock that had been produced by a provincial company, Church of Norwich, rather than by one of the leading London makers of the day.

'The clock was fitted with three trains [the interconnecting series of wheels and pinions that is used to transmit power from the mainspring to the escape mechanism and to the hands] for going, striking and quarter chiming,' commented Richard, and the clock did more than just tell the time. 'A third hand moved concentrically to show the date within the chapter ring. In the arch were twin subsidiary dials, whose purpose was to switch off the strike or the chimes, and above those there was a larger dial containing a rotating ivory ball to indicate the phase and age of the moon. The blue disc behind this larger dial revolved to tell the high tide on the local river.'

'The use of both revolving and rotating indications within such a small dial is highly unusual on a bracket clock,' Richard added, 'and is seldom even seen on longcase clocks. A sophisticated piece like this would probably have been made for a merchant whose livelihood depended on tide times so that he could gauge exactly when his goods could be shipped down Norfolk's River Yare to Yarmouth and out to the North Sea.'

The case of this bracket clock is ebony veneered (a practice that was introduced during the same period, c.1670, in which olive- and walnut-cased clocks were first produced); the hour hand is elaborate, the minute hand simpler. However, early clocks of this type were made with square dials, so the arched dial on this example is an indication that it was made during the late 18th century. Following its appearance on the *Roadshow*, the clock has gained in value. 'Good English bracket clocks have come on very strongly in the past three years,' explains Richard, 'which is why I feel quite confident that this one has more than doubled in value since I saw it.'

English bracket clocks

After the mid-17th century the spring-driven mechanism was developed – a significant advance, as this made it possible to carry a clock around for the first time. Before this period the majority of clocks had been made to be hung on the wall and, because their mechanism was weight-driven, they were not portable. The new clocks – which began to be produced from around 1660 onwards (approximately the same time as the first longcase clocks) – were fitted with short pendulums and were designed to stand on tables or on brackets that were fixed to walls. In these examples the steel spring is coiled in a barrel and unwinds as the force gradually lessens. A conical spool, which is known as the 'fusee', controls the power of the spring so that it provides the same output of power when it is almost wound down as when it is fully wound. The result is good timekeeping.

Gold pocket watch

Found at Michelham Priory, 1996; valued at £25,000. Current value up to £35,000.

When there is no documentary evidence, the facts surrounding how particular objects came into the possession of families, how much was paid for them and how they were handed down can become unclear over the years. However, this was not the case with this extremely rare English gold pocket watch, because the owners still had the original receipt. It was bought in 1920 from the Sheffield Goldsmiths' Company for £77 8s 6d (£77.46), which was a considerable sum in those days.

The original owner bought the watch to replace one stolen from him at the races. The family were wire-drawers, making the wire for watch springs exported to Switzerland, so there is a good chance, says Simon Bull, that the purchaser knew exactly what he was buying. What makes the watch so special is that it contains a *tourbillon* (the French word meaning

'whirlpool' or 'whirlwind') mechanism that rectifies the timekeeping errors of the watch caused by its wearer's movements.

'As you moved about and your watch changed position constantly – this caused minute fluctuations in timekeeping,' Simon explained. 'The best way to counteract that was to make the escapement revolve continually, to compensate for movement. They were highly complicated and difficult mechanisms to make, requiring the very highest watchmaking skills, with every step being done by hand.'

A watch such as this would only ever have been made to order for a particular customer. The Sheffield Goldsmiths' Company, the original retailer, was the best jeweller in that city, supplying high-quality items to the wealthiest families. Sadly, it transpired that the first owner died shortly after buying the watch, apparently without ever having had the chance to wear it.

Top English watch makers

As Simon Bull explained to the owners of the gold pocket watch shown here, the high value of the piece is not a consequence of its great age – for it was produced only during the early years of the 20th century. The significance of watches such as this lies in the technical superiority as well as the rarity of the sophisticated *tourbillon* mechanism. Indeed, only a very small handful of the companies that were operating at the time would have been capable of producing a watch of this extremely fine quality. They included Frodsham, Bent, S Smith & Son, Nicole Nielsen and Victor Kullberg – most of which were small firms based in London. Each of these companies employed highly skilled craftsmen in its workshops, and none of them ever signed any of the objects that they produced.

Audemar Piguet wristwatch

Found in Stowmarket, 1990; valued at £50,000. Current value £57,000.

In many cases, pieces that have been handed down through families hold the greatest surprises. This is largely because the owners tend to keep them tucked away in their homes, and may never have thought of having them valued until the *Roadshow* comes to town.

The owners of this exceptionally rare white-gold-cased minute-repeating wristwatch, made in the 1930s, knew that it was a good example and thought that it might be worth around £5,000. Simon Bull had the pleasure of confidently advising them to add a nought to their estimate. He was also able to tell them that, because it had been recased to order in a square case, it was absolutely unique: there was probably no other quite like it in existence. It sold in 1991 for £57,000.

The watch was specially made for Gubelin Lucerne, a family firm of jewellers that, with its four shops in Switzerland,

is still thriving today. The company has always been first and foremost a jewellers, but it also has a tradition of selling high-quality watches. It would have asked only the very best watch makers to engineer a piece like this. The ultra-slim case, the minute-repeating facility and the quality of the construction informed Simon that this piece had been made by Audemar Piguet, a company among the top three Swiss watch makers, along with Patek Philippe and Vacheron & Constantin.

Wristwatches were first popularized during the First World War, when the need arose for soldiers to consult watches that were more accessible than pocket watches on chains. Initially small fob watches were converted by the addition of strap fittings; by the 1920s, however, the manufacturers realized that the pocket watch was fast becoming redundant and began to produce wristwatches in significant numbers.

Audemar Piguet

Established in 1875 in the village of Le Brassus, near Geneva, Switzerland, by Eduard-Auguste Piguet and Jules-Louis Audemar, Audemar Piguet is the only watch company still to have members of the original family on its board. Jasmine Audemar, the president, is a direct descendant of Jules-Louis Audemar. The two talented young watch makers, who were both only 23 when they founded the company, set out to make complicated watch movements of exceptional quality. They began to manufacture wristwatches early in the 20th century, producing their first minute-repeater watch – which was one of the earliest – in 1907 for a man called Shaeffer, President of the Allied Chemical Corporation in New Jersey. It was bought back by the family at Sotheby's in New York in 1989 and is now housed in the Audemar Piguet museum at Le Brassus.

Pair of library globes

Found at Darlington, 1990; valued at £30,000 the pair. Current value up to £65,000.

In the days when groups of wealthy gentlemen gathered at their clubs and in one another's homes to discuss the latest voyage of discovery or the newest development in science, a large pair of globes, one terrestrial and one celestial, on handsome stands was an essential piece of furniture for the library, no less important than a writing table and comfortable chairs.

As the discussion went on late into the night, the globes slowly revolved. The terrestrial globe was consulted on matters relating to the earth and the journeys of the great explorers, while the celestial globe was studied on questions of the movement of the heavens. During the daylight hours library globes were used for educational purposes by the children of the house, working with their tutor. If the household did not possess a pair, the tutor brought his pocket globe with him.

The owner of this elegant Regency pair brought the globes to the *Roadshow* at Darlington on behalf of his father-in-law. The latter had inherited them from his father, who had bought them 40 years earlier in a sale in the south of England. They were insured for £5,000, and it was a shocked son-in-law who prepared to return home and reveal their true worth.

The maps are by Cary, one of a number of leading makers of globes in London at this time. Made in 1828, the paper maps were pasted over the original ones of 1816 – a common way of updating globes as voyages of discovery took place. Although in good condition, they needed some dry stripping to restore the original glorious colour. The globes still revolved well, an important feature for collectors. The stands resemble rosewood, but are in fact beech painted to simulate rosewood, a fashionable decorative effect of the Regency period.

The construction of globes

A pair of library globes combined the skills of two quite separate sets of craftsmen: the globe maker and the furniture maker. However, globes had been constructed for a very long time before they began to be mounted on stands. Very early examples, dating from antiquity, were carved in marble, and some Islamic celestial globes were engraved on hollow metal spheres. However, most globes dating from the 16th to the early 20th century were made from papier mâché covered with a layer of plaster, onto which 12 separate sections, or 'gores', of engraved paper maps were pasted. Map makers working in London in the late 17th century began to realize that there was money in globe making, and a thriving industry grew up. The 18th and early 19th centuries were the high point of British globe making, of which this pair is a fine example.

W & S Jones orrery

Found in Stafford, 1990; valued at £25–35,000. Current value the same.

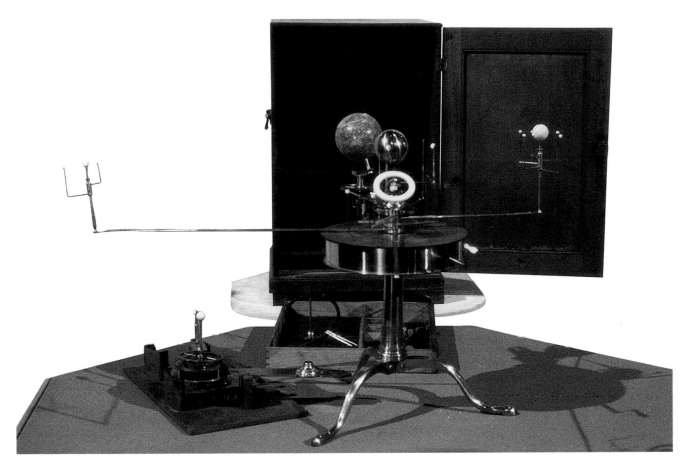

Hilary Kay generally expects to have a number of scientific instruments brought into a *Roadshow* – they are often collected by professionals who are interested in the history of the field in which they work. However, she was delighted one afternoon to come across this fine Regency orrery (a clockwork model of the solar system) by a top London firm, W & S Jones. The lacquer on the brass of the orrery was original, a fact that was vital in assessing the piece's value. Other good signs were the survival of the original carrying-case virtually intact, and the fact that only one or two of the ivory planets were missing.

Orreries – which are also known as planetariums – took their name from the fourth Earl of Cork and Orrery, who commissioned one from the manufacturer John Rowley during the early 18th century. 'They were an 18th-century gentleman's plaything, and a very expensive one at

that,' commented Hilary. 'Science at that time [during the period of fascination with the natural world and all things scientific, known as the Age of Enlightenment] was a hobby for those with the time on their hands to discuss the latest developments and discoveries. Owning something like this orrery would certainly have given a gentleman tremendous social kudos, but it was not an accurate scientific instrument.'

In the circular drum section, which rests on the single column above the tripod support, a geared mechanism turns the arms holding the planets and moon in orbit around a central pivot. There is also an engraved brass calendar plate on the surface. 'You could deconstruct it, remove the solar system and attach just the earth and the moon to show the phases of the moon,' Hilary explained. 'It really was the rich man's state-of-the-art demonstration apparatus of its day.'

W & S Jones

The brothers William and Samuel Jones took over their father's business – which had been established in 1765 – and they would continue to run the company successfully well into the 19th century. The business was based on Holborn Hill in central London. William and Samuel manufactured a wide variety of the scientific instruments being employed by scientists and hobbyists during the burgeoning age of discovery and interest in the natural world; these instruments included balances, measures, compasses, barometers, sun dials and microscopes. The globe for the firm's orrery was produced elsewhere, by the Cary brothers: John (c.1754–1825) and William (1759–1825). The business run by the brothers, who were among the foremost map and globe sellers in London in the late 18th and early 19th centuries, was based at 181 The Strand and, after 1820, at 66 St James's Street.

Powell & Lealand microscope

Found in Stoke-on-Trent, 1993; valued at £21,000. Current value up to £25,000.

It was a microscope that first sparked Hilary Kay's interest in antiques in her childhood (see page 39), and because that same microscope led to her career in the world of the auction house she is always delighted to come across one during a *Roadshow*. This example, which was manufactured in 1842 by Powell & Lealand, was an exceptional find and represented the pinnacle of 19th-century scientific instrument making.

The owner's great-great-uncle paid 30 shillings (the equivalent of £1.50 today) for the microscope. Unfortunately the owner did not know exactly when the purchase was made, but for this paltry sum his great-great-uncle received not only the microscope, but also a huge range of fascinating accessories, including an insect holder that Hilary described at the time as looking like a receptacle that should be used to store pickled onions. The lovely original lacquer on the gleaming brass is still intact on the microscope, and this, along with the number of accessories supplied with it, added to the value.

A similar microscope sold in 1992 for a world record of £25,000. This example, however, had more accessories, and Hilary advised the owner to insure it for between £35,000 and £40,000, although its auction value was around £21,000.

The earliest microscopes, which had a single lens, were made in the 16th century. Two centuries later the lenses were a great deal more powerful and were used for experiments such as looking at the circulation of the blood beneath the skin of fish. During this period of the 18th century – which is familiarly known as the Age of Enlightenment – many important scientific discoveries were made. Amateur gentlemen scientists with time and money on their hands invested in the latest scientific

instruments, such as globes, telescopes and microscopes, and used them to find out more about the world.

By the time this microscope was made, in the mid-19th century, science had moved on, and enormous advances had been made in investigating both the cause of and cure for various diseases. This example was the leading medical research microscope of its day, produced by the foremost British maker. In his book *Le Microscope* (1891) Henry van Heurck commented: 'Messrs Powell & Lealand occupy quite a unique position in the microscopic world. Their workshops are very small, the number of instruments which they produce are very few, but every piece of apparatus … is an artistic production, perfect in all its details.'

Powell & Lealand

Hugh Powell (1799–1883) set up his company in London in 1840 and began to sign microscopes with his own name. In 1842 he went into partnership with his brother-in-law, Peter Lealand, and from that time they signed their instruments 'Powell & Lealand'. Nearly all of their microscopes also showed the date of manufacture and the company's address. From 1842 to 1846 the two men operated at 24 Clarendon Street, and from 1846 to 1857 at 4 Seymour Place. In 1857, when the new Euston Road replaced a number of existing streets, among them Seymour Place, their address became 170 Euston Road. Hugh Powell was elected a founder member of the Microscopical Society of London in 1840, and Peter Lealand followed him two years later. After Hugh's death his son Thomas took over the business until it finally ceased trading in 1914.

The voyages of Captain Cook

Found in Ashford, 1993; valued at £7,500–£8,000. Current value £15–20,000.

In Britain's long naval history, few figures have captured the imagination as vividly as Captain James Cook. Expert Clive Farahar was therefore delighted to see an example of the complete official account of Cook's voyages, including all the plates from the large folio atlas that accompanied it. The volumes belonged to the owner's father-in-law, who had been given them as a present on his retirement. 'The first voyage and the third voyage were in three volumes and the second was in two,' said Clive. The first five volumes were published during Cook's lifetime, the last three posthumously.

'The captain's notes as well as those of other senior officers make up the text, with copperplate engravings serving to illustrate the journeys. Other people had gone round the world, including Drake and Hawkins in the 16th century. The 17th century saw very little important exploration, and then, in the 18th century, Cook gave us a picture of the opposite side of the world. He was the first person to chart Australia and New Zealand, and was the first to chronicle the crossing of the Antarctic Circle.'

At the time it was thought that Australia was joined to a bigger continent, and it was part of Cook's brief to confirm or refute the claims. 'He was sent by the Admiralty on all three voyages,' Clive explained. 'He came from Whitby, the son of a master collier, and came up through the ranks of the navy – an extraordinary achievement in those days. He was a tough captain, but concerned for the health of the seamen under him. He made sure they had citrus fruit to eat on board, and he lost very few through scurvy. It was wonderful to see such a complete account, but, in fact, they are not all that rare. These volumes had replacement 19th-century calf bindings, but examples with the original 18th-century calf bindings still intact are worth twice as much.'

Cook's voyages

On his pioneering first expedition (1768–71) Captain Cook, who was born in 1728 in North Yorkshire, sailed the *Endeavour* to the Pacific. He carried with him a party from the Royal Society whose members wished to observe the movement of Venus across the sun. During the voyage he circumnavigated New Zealand and charted parts of Australia for the first time. On his second expedition (1772–5) Cook circumnavigated Antarctica, discovered several Pacific island groups, which included South Sandwich Island, and annexed South Georgia. Cook's mission on his final expedition (1776–9) was to find a north-west passage connecting the north Atlantic to the north Pacific. Having failed in this quest he sailed to Hawaii to refit, and while there was killed by natives in a skirmish.

Lewis Carroll collection

**Found at Blenheim Palace, Oxfordshire, 1994, and in Oxford, 1997; valued at £50–60,000.
Current value £150,000 including letters and photographs.**

As if the thrill of seeing so many Lewis Carroll first editions at Blenheim were not enough, Clive Farahar had the pleasure of meeting the owner again at Christ Church, Oxford, the author's own college, three years later. This time, letters and photographs had been added to the collection.

'It was the sheer quantity and quality of the collection that was extraordinary,' said Clive. 'As a child the owner's aunt knew Carroll. It is possible that she was one of his little girls. All the volumes were presentation copies, signed by the author in the lilac ink that he always used.' The owner had copies of *Alice's Adventures in Wonderland* and *Through the Looking-Glass* translated into French, Dutch and German.

'He also had *The Hunting of the Snark*, *Phantasmagoria* and *Sylvie and Bruno*,' said Clive, 'but *Wonderland* and *Through the Looking-Glass* are the books that have really captured people's imaginations – and the exciting aspect was that everything

was pristine. I thought the collection might be worth £50–60,000, but once I had seen the letters written by Carroll to the owner's aunt, Annie Rogers, and the photos, I upped the value considerably.'

The first 50 or so copies of *Alice's Adventures in Wonderland* were issued in July 1865, but the reproduction quality was poor; a second edition came out that November. The unbound sheets of the first edition were shipped to America, given a new frontispiece and issued in 1866. *Alice* was an immediate success, appearing in several languages. The sequel, *Through The Looking-Glass and What Alice Found There*, was published in 1871.

Lewis Carroll

Charles Lutwidge Dodgson was born in 1832, the son of the Rector of Daresbury in Cheshire and the third of eleven children. Educated at Rugby, he arrived at Christ Church, Oxford, in 1851 and graduated in 1855, when he was appointed Sub-Librarian of the college with which he was to be associated for the rest of his life. Although he earned his living as a lecturer in mathematics, he began writing poetry and prose in 1845, and in 1856 started to use the pseudonym Lewis Carroll. In July 1862 an entry in his diary reads: 'I made an expedition up the river to Godstow with the three Liddells; we had tea on the bank there, and did not reach Christ Church again till half past eight.' This may be the first indication of the telling of *Alice's Adventures in Wonderland*, one of the most important books in the history of children's fiction. Carroll, as he is now remembered, died in 1898.

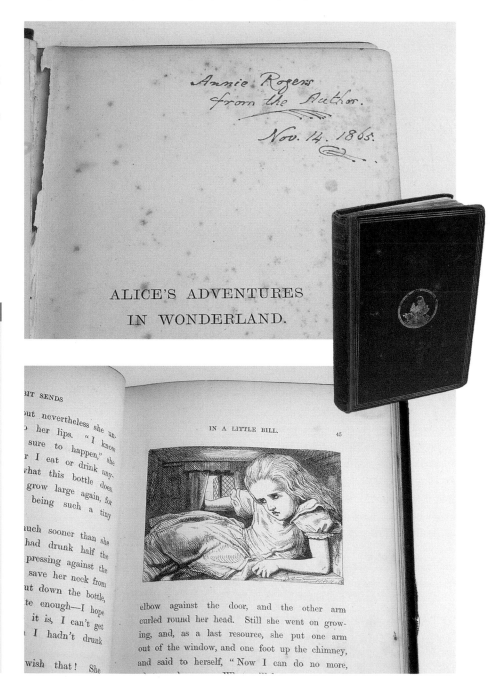

Photographs of Scott's Antarctic expedition

Found in Bolton, 1997; valued at £4–5,000. Current value the same.

Expert Hugh Bett, relatively new to the team, was aware of the competition to acquire photographs of the Antarctic taken during the early part of the 20th century. He was delighted, therefore, to find this portfolio and astonished to hear how it came into the owners' possession.

Working in housing development around 30 years ago, the owner and his wife spent part of a weekend in the garden of a large house that was about to be demolished. 'We were considering taking some of the plants before the bulldozers moved in,' he said, 'when we noticed what looked like the back of a large picture frame leaning in a corner up against a wall. When we picked it up, we found these photographs.'

Taken by official photographer Herbert Ponting, the photographs were shot at base camp and show each of the men on Scott's famous expedition to conquer the South Pole, which left England on 1 June 1910.

One very poignant image stood out – a group of all five members of the expedition taken at the South Pole. 'Scott desperately wanted to be the first there and arrived to find they had been beaten by the Norwegian Captain Roald Amundsen,' said Hugh. 'This is the most famous of all the images, found undeveloped in the camera in the tent with the bodies on 10 February 1913. They died on the way back, 11 miles [18km] from base camp.' This shot was taken by Birdie Bowers (seated front left), and a string leading from his hand to the camera is just visible.

On his return to England, Ponting held an exhibition of the photographs, and several portfolios went on to be issued. 'The value of individual photographs varies according to condition. These sepia prints are in fair condition, but the fact that they are in this portfolio means they have a lot more going for them,' said Hugh 'The portfolios are very rare. I've only ever seen one other.'

Scott of the Antarctic

Robert Falcon Scott, one of the greatest figures of polar exploration through the ages, has perhaps captured the public imagination more than any other explorer. He was born on 6 June 1868 in Devonport, Devon, and joined the Royal Navy at the age of 14. He was placed in command of the first National Antarctic expedition in 1900, returning in 1904 after having established a land base on the shores of McMurdo Sound, explored the area to the east of the Ross Ice Shelf and named Edward VII Peninsula. The second expedition was the one that ended in tragedy for the entire party. Among Scott's diaries and notebooks were the words: 'Had we lived I should have had a tale to tell of the hardihood, endurance and courage of my companions which would have stirred the heart of every Englishman. These rough notes and our dead bodies must tell the tale.'

Chinese stamp

Discovered at the Science Museum, 1993; valued at £5,000. Current value up to £10,000.

Not surprisingly, Tony Banwell sees dozens of stamp albums during the children's *Roadshows*, for stamps have been a favourite area of collecting among children for generations. When Ben Ward sat down at his table at the Science Museum in 1993, Tony had no reason to suspect that his collection would be any different from the majority – in other words, well loved and put together with great care, but worth little in monetary terms.

As he turned the sparsely filled album pages, however, Tony was rewarded by a sight that he has very little expectation of seeing in his day-to-day business as a stamp specialist at Sotheby's, far less on a children's *Roadshow*. In the album – which had been given to him by his great-aunt – Ben had a very rare China 1885 3 Candarins stamp.

'It had this extraordinary number "3" before the "Candarin",' said Tony. 'It was put in as an experiment, and we don't know the reason why. It must have been some sort of trial, because it was issued just before the smaller version of this stamp came out, so they were probably playing around with ideas. After the publicity surrounding the appearance of Ben's stamp on the *Roadshow*, six more have since been discovered. We now think that one sheet of 25 stamps may have been released with the flaw, so there may be others still in existence.'

Ben's family was also able to confirm that an uncle of his father had served in China with a cavalry regiment. The stamp album had been handed down through the generations, and had lain untouched for many years.

The find caused such a stir on the international market that it is now referred to by philatelists everywhere as the 'South Kensington Small 3' and was written about in the *Wall Street Journal* as well as in Britain's daily newspapers. Ben Ward became one of the most famous schoolboys of the moment. The stamp was put up for auction at Sotheby's in 1994 and reached £5,700. Ben spent part of the rich reward on a state-of-the-art computer.

The 1970s saw an unprecedented boom in the popularity of Chinese stamps. Pockets of wealth began to accumulate on the Chinese mainland and in a more concentrated form in Hong Kong and Taiwan. Within a few years the reversal of the flow of the past 150 years had turned into a flood. In 1991 a Chinese collector paid £374,000 at auction for a sheet of 25 stamps from the same issue as Ben's, and today nearly every major collection of Chinese stamps is held in the East.

Chinese stamps

The postal service used in China today is one of the oldest in the world. It was talked about in admiring terms by the explorer Marco Polo (1254–1324) after his return from the East in the late 13th century (although postal networks have operated in Europe, often on an international scale, since the Middle Ages, when they were set up by guilds, merchants and centres of academic scholarship). Chinese collectors have always valued rare stamps and wished to buy their own examples, but until recently the country's political climate and a lack of spending power led to almost all rare Chinese stamps being purchased by overseas collectors. Since the collapse of the Cultural Revolution, and with the attendant opportunities for individual wealth, this situation has been completely reversed. Chinese collectors are now among the most enthusiastic and prolific of all.

Lloyd's Patriotic Fund sword

Found in Ipswich, 1985; valued at £8–9,000. Current value £18,000.

It had been a fairly quiet day at the *Roadshow* for Roy Butler. As the crowds started to dwindle towards the end of the afternoon, he decided to take a break from his table and was walking across the hall when he saw a gentleman coming towards him with the lion's head of the sword shown above protruding from a carrier bag. 'I knew at once what it was,' Roy explained afterwards. 'I said to the man, "I think you're looking for me", and we recorded the piece late in the day. It made a perfect end to the proceedings.'

Swords such as this one were given as honorary awards by the Lloyd's Patriotic Fund to officers who had served at the Battle of Trafalgar. The Committee of the Patriotic Fund met on 3 December 1805 and decided that swords to the value of £100 each – then a considerable sum – should be presented to surviving captains and to commanders of His Majesty's ships who had been involved in the action. Swords worth £50 (of which this picture is an example) and some worth £30 were awarded to certain other officers, and it was one of the former that Roy found himself examining at Ipswich.

The elaborate swords, each one of which was inscribed for the recipient, were intended to be worn only with full dress at official functions or if the recipient was sitting for his portrait. There is a fine painting of Sir Philip Durham, captain of the *Defiance* at Trafalgar, with his sword proudly at his side, in the National Maritime Museum at Greenwich. These swords are decorative and impressive to look at, but would have been flimsy and clumsy as fighting weapons. Maker Richard Teed supplied 153 swords, 56 worth £100, 82 worth £50, and 15 worth £30.

Officers were given the option of choosing a silver vase made by Rundell, Bridge & Rundell rather than the sword, and some preferred the former, which could be displayed as a trophy. The vases that belonged to Captain Edward Rotheram, flag-captain of the *Royal Sovereign*, and Captain Capel of the frigate *Phoebe* are now in the splendid Nelson Collection at Lloyd's in the City of London (the collection also includes one of the honorary swords). Others are kept at the Maritime Museum at Greenwich and the Royal United Service Institution, while some, such as the one seen at Ipswich, remain in private hands.

Lloyd's Patriotic Fund

Lloyd's Patriotic Fund is the oldest British fund of its kind still in existence today. The Fund was inaugurated at a meeting held on 20 July 1803 at Lloyd's Coffee House, a renowned centre of gentlemanly discourse, in the Royal Exchange in London. Two months before this meeting took place, war between Britain and France had broken out once again after the uneasy peace which had followed the signing of the Treaty of Amiens in 1802. As a result patriotic fervour in the country was at its height, and the Fund's committee had few problems in entreating both companies and individuals to contribute to its noble cause. Donations poured into the coffers, and by March 1804 a grand total of over £179,000 had been received. The committee was therefore able to grant sums of money to those servicemen who had been wounded in action against the French, as well as to bestow annuities on the dependants of those who had been killed in the war. A further use of the Fund was to give rewards in the form of money, or a sword such as the one shown here (or a silver vase if the recipient preferred) to those who had fought so heroically against the French.

Army gold medal

Found at Michelham Priory, 1996; valued at £8,000. Current value £8,500.

Roy Butler felt almost humbled when this large British Army Gold Medal was put into his hands. 'I've seen these before,' he said, 'but I've never actually had the privilege of handling one. So few were awarded by the Government that they are extremely rare. They were given during the Peninsular War of 1808–14 and the war of 1812.' The proud owner was a direct descendant of Major-General Frederick Maitland, who fought against the French at Martinique in 1809.

Some of the first of these medals were given to the 13 officers who had formed part of a small British force under Major-General Sir John Stuart, who defeated the French at the battle of Maida in Calabria, southern Italy. They were small gold medals, measuring 38mm (1½in) in diameter, with the head of George III on the obverse and inscribed 'Geogius Tertius Rex'. On the reverse was the figure of Britannia; she was casting a spear with her right hand, and on her left arm was the Union shield.

By 1810 it had been decided to award medals of one size with the battle's name engraved (though that for Barossa was die-struck) on the reverse. Medals were struck to commemorate the battles of Roleia and Vimiera, the cavalry operations at Sahagun and Benevente and the battles of Corunna and Talavera in Spain in 1808 and 1809.

The large medal, of which this is an example, is 54mm (2⅛in) in diameter. On the obverse is the figure of Britannia seated on a globe. She is wearing a helmet, and holds a laurel wreath in her right hand and a palm branch in her left. Beside her is the head of the British lion, and her left hand rests on a shield charged with the crosses of the Union. On the reverse is the name of the engagement – in this case 'Martinique'. It hung from a ring and was worn around the neck suspended from a crimson ribbon with blue edges. The smaller medal was made to exactly the same design, but was to be worn from the buttonhole. Production of both medals ceased when the Companionship of the Bath was instituted in 1814.

Military medals

Although officers had been rewarded for their bravery, the first medal to be issued to every man who served, regardless of rank, was the silver Waterloo Medal of 1815. The war against France had rumbled on from 1793 until 1815, and those soldiers who had gone to Spain and Portugal to fight the French in the Peninsular War of 1808–14 felt very disgruntled about the recognition of their naval compatriots' bravery when they themselves returned home empty-handed. This continued until Queen Victoria decided, in 1848, to institute a General Service Medal to every man who had fought in the Peninsular War. However, there were no posthumous awards – only survivors could receive a medal, and for every battle fought one bar across the ribbon was awarded. The GSMs with several bars across, showing that one man survived many encounters over several years, can be worth over £1,000, while a medal bearing only one bar for one of the more obscure battles may have a value of £6–700.

Embroidered casket

Found in Cheltenham, 1995; valued at £15–25,000. Current value £28,500.

Victoria Leatham, as curator of the collection at Burghley House in Stamford, Lincolnshire, is very well acquainted with the type of embroidered casket that was brought to the *Roadshow* when it visited Cheltenham, Gloucestershire. The owner had inherited the casket ten years previously, when it had been valued at approximately £3,000, but otherwise knew very little about it.

It represented a very good example of late-17th-century embroidery, and was produced during the reign of Charles II; the needlework carried out at this time by women at home in the wealthy households of England is considered to be some of the finest in existence. These embroidered caskets still come to light and always fetch many thousands of pounds at auction – particularly when they have survived in good condition through the years, as this one had done.

'When new, the colours would have been quite brilliant and garish, the sort of thing we would actually consider rather vulgar today', said Victoria. The wooden carcass of the casket is covered with panels of embroidery, which would have been separately worked in silk threads before being attached to the piece and then banded with silver thread. The lady of the household would have asked the estate carpenter to make up the chest, complete with drawers and a domed cover; the latter was designed to lift up, revealing a well for storing small objects.

'Pieces like this served as portable desks as well as jewellery boxes and vanity cases,' Victoria added. Sometimes caskets of this type also incorporate secret compartments. These are accessed by pressing hidden buttons, and ladies could use them to hide love-letters in the process of being written, or those sent to them by admirers.

Stuart embroidery

The Stuart period encompassed the reigns of seven monarchs, from James I, who acceded in 1603, to Queen Anne, who died in 1714, with the drab Commonwealth sandwiched between Charles I and Charles II. Needlework became decidedly more opulent with the Restoration of the monarchy in 1660, the period when this casket was made. The mistresses of well-to-do households organized the gentlewomen and children under their authority in various projects to enhance the comfort of draughty rooms, including making samplers, bed hangings, coverlets and cushions. The best materials – gold and silver wire threads, silks, ribbons and laces in glorious colours – were bought from merchants. These were transformed into the animals, insects, flowers and figures that feature in work of this period, inspired by the well-tended gardens around the house and by Bible stories.

Mid-18th-century silk-brocade shoes

Found at Windermere, 1995; valued at £4–5,000. Current value the same.

Of all the antiques in existence today, costumes and textiles are, inevitably, especially vulnerable to damage and to the passage of time. For this reason it is always a delightful surprise to come across something that is still in wonderful condition after 350 years, and which tells us so much about how the original owner lived. At the *Roadshow* in Windermere, Hilary Kay fell upon these mid-18th-century silk-brocade shoes with alacrity as soon as she saw them among various other pieces of antique costume and textiles.

The owner thinks that the shoes must have belonged to her great-great-grandmother because their soles are marked 'Petty', which was her mother's maiden name. She found them when she was packing up belongings ready to move from a house in which the family had lived for several hundred years.

Fortunately, and to Hilary Kay's delight, the shoes had obviously been carefully wrapped and stored, and kept away both from direct light and from any damp. As a result their colours had remained wonderfully bright, while the exquisite stitching on them was still completely

intact. Remarkably, too, the pattens – a type of leather clog intended to be worn as protective overshoes – were still with them. The pattens' survival made the shoes an extremely rare and even more desirable collector's item.

A wealthy noblewoman would have had the shoes made, probably to match an opulent open robe ordered for a special occasion such as a wedding or a grand event at court. The slightly rounded toes on this pair are a change from the very pointed shoes that were in vogue earlier in the century. Originally the front of each shoe would probably also have been covered with a buckle. At the beginning of the century buckles were quite small and square, but they became larger and more ostentatious over a number of years.

Pattens were often made with wooden soles for practicality. They were designed to be worn outside in the streets, to lift the wearer's delicate shoes safely away from any mud or dust, although the lady who wore this pair seems unlikely ever to have set foot in the mire. To have had the pattens covered in the same silk as the shoes would have been considered – at that time – the ultimate fashion statement.

Mid-18th-century costume

Costume trends and fashions among the wider populace during the 18th century were still greatly influenced by what was happening at court. However, the Hanoverian kings (George I–IV) and their queens were rather stuffy in their dress tastes (George IV is something of an exception), so any ladies of fashion who wished to cause a stir among their contemporaries generally took their inspiration from what was currently in vogue in Paris. Fashion dolls, daintily dressed in miniature versions of the latest Parisian styles, were shipped across the Channel, and the gowns were then made up for their English recipients – often by French seamstresses, tailors and milliners plying their trade in London. The owner of the embroidered shoes shown here would probably have worn them with an open-fronted gown and an elaborate petticoat underneath. To the front of the gown would have been fitted a beautiful (and separate) stomacher, as was the custom at that period. This part of a lady's dress was triangular in shape and was usually embroidered and/or laced with ribbons for added decorative effect.

Carved wooden doll

Found in Ashford, 1993; valued at £10–15,000. Current value the same or slightly lower.

Bunny Campione can be certain of seeing many dolls at every *Roadshow* she attends – usually they are the much-loved relics of childhood that have been stored away in attics or at the top of wardrobes and brought out especially for the occasion. It is rare, however, for good-quality 18th-century carved wooden dolls to make an appearance. The example shown here, which was manufactured around 1760–70, had come down through the male line of a family. This was an unusual provenance because dolls are, as one would expect, generally passed on from mother to daughter.

Although wooden dolls were being made in Germany during the 18th century, this example is typically English, with her dotted eyebrows and lashes, fork fingers and square, crudely pinned hips. The wig is made of real hair, which would have first been attached to a cotton latticework base, and then somewhat inelegantly nailed onto her head. Typically for a doll originating from this period, she has enamel, pupil-less eyes.

Dolls such as this one often suffer from some damage over the years, and are rarely found in absolutely perfect condition. The tip of this doll's dainty nose is very slightly chipped, but otherwise she is in remarkably good condition. 'It is amazing that her striped silk-taffeta dress and her little slippers have survived so well,' said Bunny. 'Underneath is a stiffened corset. These were rich little girls' playthings, and the costumes were faithfully copied from the mothers' wardrobes.'

Dolls at this time were turned on a lathe, before being carved and finished by the same person. 'We don't really know who produced them, but they may have been done by craftsmen who also made furniture,' Bunny added. 'The lovely thing about them is that, because they were made individually, each one has a different expression. Some look remarkably similar, which probably means that they were made by the same craftsman. Once the carving was finished they were covered with a layer of gesso and painted.'

Good-quality carved wooden dolls like this one were made in the hundreds rather than in the thousands during the 18th century. Even so, the marketability and commercial value of the dolls is rather uncertain at the moment, because a number of the world's major collectors have either died or appear to have stopped buying. The consequence is that, unless a fresh and devoted new group of collectors with plentiful funds springs up to replace them, the value of such dolls is very likely to fall.

Carved wooden dolls

If you come across one of these dolls, bear in mind that there are several characteristics that distinguish early examples from those manufactured after 1780 and into the 19th century. Late-17th-century dolls have painted eyes, whereas by the start of the 18th century enamel, pupil-less eyes began to appear. This doll has long fork fingers; by the end of the 18th century fingers had become shorter and more primitive-looking. Some early examples have rounded hips; late-18th-century dolls have no waist, slimmer necks and a more pronounced slope to the shoulders, possibly in response to the changing fashion in clothes. By the 19th century, when dolls were being produced in greater quantities and with less care, the faces were often more crudely painted and the legs rather less shapely.

Gustave Vichy automaton

Found in Bognor Regis, 1980; valued at £3–5,000. Sold at Sotheby's in 1996 for £84,000.

This very rare Gustave Vichy bird-trainer automaton, made c.1895, has always been fondly known by his owner as 'Charles'. Her grandfather bought him as a present for his daughter in a house sale in Kent in 1897 for £3 10s. (£3.50). When the elderly gentleman died in 1926, Charles was bought by the family from the sale of his effects for £7, and he remained with them until he was sold at Sotheby's in 1996 for £84,000.

This was one of the great finds during the early days of the *Roadshow*. Arthur Negus, who was still involved with the show at that stage, was absolutely fascinated by Charles and his antics. Hilary Kay was only 23 at the time and, by her own admission, still learning. She had handled other automata, but had never seen anything so fine, and knew instinctively that Charles was a unique piece. 'He was not the only one made, but these pieces are so fragile, and there are so many things that can go wrong with them, that I knew he was extremely rare in this condition,' said Hilary. In fact

the only other known example in such wonderful condition is part of the famous Murtogh D Guinness Collection, which is housed in New York.

Charles survives resplendent in his original, pristine midnight-blue velvet doublet, hose, cape and beret faced with rose-pink satin. His costume is appliquéd with fruit motifs, his cuffs are made of the finest lace and he stands holding a feathered bird in his left hand. When activated he brings a flute up to his mouth and plays with articulated fingers

to the accompaniment of a cylinder musical movement. The bird then moves his head and beak, and sings back the tune that it has learned from the flautist.

The chief wish of Charles's owner, when the automaton was put up for sale, was that he should go to someone who would love and appreciate him as much as she had always done. She need not have worried on this account, as only a truly dedicated collector would have been prepared to pay the princely sum that Charles eventually fetched at auction.

Gustave Vichy

Legend has it that by the time Gustave Vichy was thinking about retiring, in 1895, he had amassed a fortune of a million-and-a-half gold francs as well as several valuable properties. He was one of the most successful 19th-century French automaton makers. The son of mechanical-toy makers Antoine and Geneviève Vichy, he was born in 1839 and began his working life in 1864 as a mechanic and clock maker in Paris, soon building a formidable reputation for his automata. His wife Thérèse dressed his figures and, as the firm flourished, guided numerous other seamstresses. The Vichys' son, Henri, born in 1866, eventually came into the business. He was highly talented, and many pieces were certainly his creations. However, when father and son fell out, at the turn of the century, Gustave abandoned his plans to retire and carried on directing the company until his death in 1904.

Chad Valley Snow White

Found in Bridlington, 1994; valued at £2,500. Current value the same.

Disney films were already loved by children – and their parents – all over Europe and in the United States by the time that *Snow White and the Seven Dwarfs* was released in 1937. Since there were huge profits to be made even in those less commercial times, toy manufacturers clamoured to obtain licences to market the various ranges of toys based on the most popular of the Disney characters. The Chad Valley Snow White set shown here was given to the owner by her parents in 1938. Her pride and joy, it did not suffer the ravages of play, but was stored carefully in a box for many years and therefore remained in very good condition.

Bunny Campione examined the set when the owner brought it along to the *Roadshow* in Humberside. Bunny had handled many of these Snow White sets over the years, but she had rarely seen a complete example of this size and in such an excellent state of repair. As she commented at the time: 'What usually happened was that a set was bought for a family that contained both boys and girls. The girls would take the Snow White doll to their hearts, while the boys played roughly with the dwarfs. As a result, the characters fell into disrepair over the years and also often became separated, so complete sets are hard to find.'

Other factors also add to the value of this particular set, Bunny explained: 'Chad Valley made them in various sizes, and this one is much larger than usual. The doll is about 36cm (14in) long and the dwarfs 18cm (7in). Snow White incorporates a lullaby that is activated by pressing her tummy. It is very uncommon to find it still in good working order, as this is; each of the dolls also still retains the Chad Valley label, further increasing their rarity. Not only that, but Snow White is still wearing her original clothes, and they are far from tattered and torn. It was a pleasure to find such a lovely example on a *Roadshow*.'

Chad Valley

Named after the Chad Valley district of Birmingham where it started up in 1860, this major British toy producer was founded by Joseph and Alfred Johnson. In 1897 the company moved to Harborne and made its name with traditional games and board games. During the 1920s it began making toys, including teddy bears and felt-covered dolls such as these. Norah Wellings, a well-known British maker of fabric dolls, worked for Chad Valley before setting up on her own. During the 1930s and after the Second World War, Chad Valley made a range of lithographed tinplate and aluminium toys and die-cast toys, including the Weekin range of clockwork toys for the Rootes Group. In 1938, the year this set was produced, the firm was granted a Royal Warrant. It went public in 1950 and took over the Chiltern Toy Works before being bought by Palitoy in 1978. Ten years ago Woolworths UK bought the right to use the name Chad Valley on its own range of toys.

Tinplate Mickey Mouse

Found in Moreton-in-Marsh, 1997; valued at £10,000. Sold at Christie's in 1997 for £51,000.

It was the end of a long, busy day when a gentleman sat down in front of Hilary Kay and unwrapped a tinplate Mickey Mouse on a motorcycle with Minnie riding pillion. It took only seconds for Hilary to realize that she was looking at something extremely special: a rare early clockwork Mickey made in Germany by Tipp & Co. The toy had been produced around 1929 and carried the manufacturer's trade mark: a 'T' intersected by a 'C'. It was brought in by the friend of a man whose uncle was given it on his ninth birthday in June 1930, and was bought at Woolworths.

The owner had obviously been either a very careful child or not terribly interested in playing with the toy, because not only was it in excellent condition, it is also thought to be one of only ten examples of the rare five-fingered Mickey motorcyclist still in existence today. This toy is very typical of early Mickeys, since it features a longer nose than those found on examples manufactured after 1935, a toothy grin and what are described as 'piecrust' eyes – in other words, eyes that are circular in shape and have had a triangular slice removed.

To add to the thrill, the toy emerged from its original box, which is decorated with a lithographed label depicting Mickey and Minnie riding the motorcycle down a country lane. It is now believed to be the only known example with its original box intact. Indeed, when the toy was sold at Christie's in 1997 for £51,000 (a figure that was considerably higher than the allotted valuation price), it was thought that the presence of the box alone might have accounted for as much as £25,000 of this amount.

Tipp & Co

The German toy company was founded in 1912 by a Miss Tipp and a Mr Carstens. After only a year Miss Tipp left and Phillip Ullmann took her place, becoming sole proprietor by 1919. During the 1920s and early 1930s the company made a wide range of good-quality tinplate toys, at a time when Germany led the field in toymaking. Clockwork vehicles such as motorcars, motorcycles and aeroplanes were their speciality, and their success continued until 1933, when Ullmann fled from Nazi Germany and went to live in England. He set up in business in south Wales and, apart from the war years of 1939–45, continued to make tinplate toys until 1971. Meanwhile in Germany the government took over Ullmann's company, placing it under the management of a former director of Bing, another successful toy firm. The company was returned to Ullmann in 1948. A range of toys continued to be made there until 1971, when the company closed down.

Mickey Mouse

Invented by Walt Disney in 1928, Mickey became one of those enviable newcomers to show business – an overnight sensation. Companies were soon vying for licences to produce Mickey in various guises and materials: from soft toys to examples in tinplate, celluloid and ceramic. Earlier in his career Disney had lost the rights to the image of his first cartoon character, Oswald the Lucky Rabbit. The experience made him determined to retain tight control on all his subsequent creations, and led to one of the most successful licensing operations of all time. Collectors today are looking for the rarest examples of Mickey Mouse that survive in the best possible condition, and this wonderful example fulfils every criterion. In the auction catalogue it carried an estimate of £15–20,000, and it eventually sold for £51,000. The market for Mickey Mouse memorabilia is truly international. An instantly recognizable icon, Disney's creation is as much loved and appreciated by children who discover him for the first time today as he was by those who encountered him in the 1930s.

Märklin tinplate biplane

Found at Chatsworth, 1996; valued at £100,000.

Hilary Kay first came across this extremely rare Märklin tinplate biplane in 1987 when she was putting together an exhibition at Sotheby's for the Save the Children Fund. She visited many large English houses, one of which was Chatsworth, in Derbyshire.

The Duchess of Devonshire didn't think that she had anything relevant to lend, but invited Hilary to look around. 'I found the biplane in one of the rooms open to the public – on an open shelf! We used it in the exhibition and, when it was returned, we suggested it deserved a more secure home. When we went to Chatsworth in 1997 to do a *Roadshow* the Duchess invited me down to the gold vaults, and there was the biplane, safely locked away.'

When Hilary talked about the biplane on the *Roadshow*, she mentioned that the only other one known used to belong to a Thai prince. After the show the programme received a letter from a lady who had been a housekeeper at the Duke of Devonshire's school. 'I wonder if you realized,' she asked, 'that the Duke and the Prince were the best of friends?' This connection was fascinating. It meant that the pair had probably gone through the sumptuous Märklin catalogue before Christmas in 1909 and had both picked out the biplane as the present that they most wanted. Luckily for them, their wishes came true.

The biplane would have been an expensive toy at the time, because it was produced by one of the most celebrated German toy manufacturers. Made of tinplate, with celluloid wings – measuring 43cm (17in) in diameter – and a celluloid propeller, it was modelled on the Wright brothers' biplane of the period. Hilary was astonished that the toy had survived in such good condition because celluloid, an early form of plastic, is a highly volatile material.

Märklin

During the 19th century tinplate was the most widely used material for toymaking, and the company of Märklin, established in 1859, became one of the best known of the renowned German manufacturers, which also included Bing and Carette. These companies produced high-quality painted tinplate toys, many only accessible to the wealthy. Märklin was based in Göppingen, producing mainly for export. Its splendid trains were often made to imitate the models of the buyers, with liveries to match, and its equally impressive ships had names and inscriptions changed according to their destination. German toy makers were hard hit by both world wars, but Märklin has survived to this day. Its boats, trains, cars and aeroplanes are sought after worldwide by collectors who appreciate the very high quality maintained by producing a limited range of toys with great attention to detail.

Favourite treasures

It's not hard to imagine the scene in homes up and down the country whenever the *Roadshow* is in town. Favourite objects get taken down from shelves, mantelpieces and walls, while long-forgotten wedding, christening and retirement presents are pulled from the backs of cupboards and hauled from lofts. Dusted down and wrapped in newspapers and tea towels, they're taken along to the *Roadshow* in the shopping bags of the nation.

For every valuable and fascinating piece that is featured on the programme, there are hundreds that don't receive the star treatment; yet these overlooked items are no less precious for all that. Each one has a special significance for the person who owns it, regardless of whether it is a postcard album, a Japanese coffee set, a press-moulded glass jug or a silver fob watch that has been passed down through a family from generation to generation.

The majority of these objects, made and bought in their thousands, were manufactured from the late 19th century onwards. These pieces tell the story of the extraordinary advances made in mass production during this period, a time when Britain was also doing brisk trade with the Far East. Decorative objects began to appear in relatively humble homes because the huge quantities in which they were produced made them affordable for the first time. Inexpensive ornaments, such as clocks, electroplated tea services and pretty coloured glass, found their way into the display cabinets and onto the mantelpieces and shelves of homes up and down the land.

As manufacturing processes became more mechanized and sophisticated, so did methods of travel. The railways grew, as did the road system; the seaside holiday or day trip became affordable, and out came the souvenirs, many of which are now eminently collectable.

The First World War generated a huge number of mementoes, many of them infused with great emotion and treasured by the relatives of men who died in the trenches. Collectively, these favourite treasures reflect the lives and histories of all the people who make the *Antiques Roadshow* compulsive viewing.

Books, prints and ephemera

▼ **Two chromolithographs, c.1930; value: £20–30 each.** On average, 40 per cent of the pictures brought to the *Roadshow* are chromolithographs (coloured pictures printed by lithography). Many owners think that they are watercolours because the ink is so faithfully applied, and in some cases they carry the signature of the artist responsible for the original. The publisher's details and blind stamp are usually around the border, but these are easily hidden by framing right up to the image. Sometimes they are glued onto canvas or hardboard to give them texture and varnished over in order to create the look of an oil painting. The colours never look right, and fade with time. The landscape on the left is signed by the artist and the portrait on the right is a Pear's (the soap manufacturer) print, which gives it a slight edge in terms of value. More usually, chromolithographs are worth £5–10 each.

**▲▼ Typical postcards,
1910–20; value: £1–5 each.** Albums filled with postcards telling of family seaside holidays, day trips and the changing face of British towns and country landscapes flood into every *Roadshow*. Their value is small in monetary terms, but their sentimental value is often beyond price.

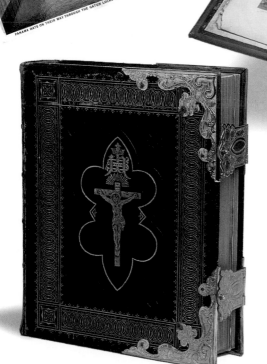

▲ *Carte de visite* album, late 19th century; value: £40–60. The early photographs that are displayed in these albums were printed in exactly the same size as calling cards, which is why they are known as *cartes de visite*. Every *Roadshow* produces its crop of these albums full of studio images of distant relatives, such as this example of a boy standing beside a carved staircase. The pages are printed with decorative scenes, and some, such as this one, are musical. In better condition it would be worth up to £80.

◄▲ Family Bible, c.1890; value: £10–15.
A place was reserved in most households for the family Bible, and many were handed down from generation to generation, for religious reasons or simply as family heirlooms. Many of them survive, and a number of these find their way to the *Roadshow*; some are in better condition than others, but few have anything other than sentimental value.

139

Jewellery

► **Cross-over ring, 1915–20; value: £60–80.** Countless young men presented rings such as this to their sweethearts before boarding the trains to do their duty in the trenches. Mounted in platinum and yellow gold, the tiny diamond at the centre is surrounded by metal, cut and faceted to look like smaller diamonds. For this reason these items are known as 'cross-over rings' with 'illusion' settings.

▼ **Two cameo rings, c.1950; value: £15–20 each.** Machine-cut in Italy around the middle of the 20th century, these mass-produced shell-cameo plaques were brought back to Britain to be mounted by jewellers. Shell cameos are highly vulnerable to wear; because they chip and crack easily, they are best made up into brooches rather than rings. The one on the left has a marcasite surround.

▲ **Rolled-gold brooch, 1885–90; value: £15–20.** Small rolled-gold (and silver) brooches were made by machine in the late 19th century and mass-produced for the mill girls of the north of England, which explains why so many of them are pierced, applied or embossed with girls' names. They were among the most affordable items of jewellery of the time. The stamps vary; this example has a horseshoe flanked by leaves and flowers.

▲ **Gold brooch, 1890–95; value: £30–40.** Simple and pretty, this late-Victorian brooch is set with two tear-shaped garnets.

◄ **Gold star and crescent brooch, c.1890; value: £75.** The jewellery expert usually sees as many as a dozen of these little late-19th-century seed pearl, star and crescent brooches during the day.

Ceramics

▼ **Octagonal Jubilee plate, 1886; value: £75–100.** Memorabilia relating to Queen Victoria's Coronation are thin on the ground and consequently much sought after. It was an event that passed without fuss; in 1838 manufacturers had yet to discover how lucrative royal commemorative items could be. By the time this plate was made for Victoria's Golden Jubilee, hundreds of thousands of plates and mugs were produced to celebrate the milestone – this is a better example, well printed and in good condition.

► **Pair of German bisque figures, c.1900; value: £60–90 the pair.** Mass-produced to adorn the mantelpieces of cottages and terraced houses the length and breadth of the British Isles, thousands of figures such as these were exported from Germany and France around the beginning of the 20th century. They are often found on plinths, covered with glass domes.

Metalwork

▲ **Britannia-metal teapot, c.1890; value: £30.**
Britannia metal, a substitute for silver, is
actually a type of pewter containing 90 per
cent tin, 8 per cent antimony and 2 per cent
copper. It was first manufactured around 1800
in Sheffield, Birmingham and London, and
objects were formed around a pattern on a
power-driven wheel. The process, known as
'spinning', produced wares that were much
thinner than cast pewter, and the material
could be die-stamped, turned and cast, which
made it ideal for mass production. Teapots
such as this one are stalwarts of the *Antiques
Roadshow*. Originally silver-plated, the plate
is usually so worn that only traces remain.

▲ **Spelter figures, late 19th century;
value: £80–100.** Spelter, a zinc alloy very
prone to damage, was used as a substitute
for bronze in all sorts of affordable objects,
including clock cases and candlesticks. These
French costume figures, with their bronzed
finish, are very typical of the kind of item that
finds its way to the Miscellaneous tables at
every *Roadshow*. In bronze, they would be
worth closer to £800.

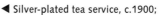

◄ **Silver-plated tea service, c.1900;
value: £100–150.** Made mainly in Sheffield
and Birmingham, silver-plated tea services
were considerably more affordable than their
solid-silver relations, which are worth closer
to £400. Electroplating, a technique in which
a base metal is covered with a thin layer of
silver by means of an electrolytic process,
was invented in 1840 by George Elkington, a
Birmingham metal worker. Many tea services
such as this have been given as wedding and
anniversary presents over the years.

Clocks and watches

▲ **Two silver pocket watches, c.1900; value: under £50 each.** When these two Swiss examples were made, every self-respecting gent owned a pocket watch. The one on the left with the ribbed knob is a manual-wind model, and the one on the right is a key-wind type. Made in great quantities and well looked after by generations of proud owners, they survive in great numbers, and those of average quality, such as these, are worth little in monetary terms. Since the invention of the wristwatch they have fallen out of use.

▶ **Gold watch chain, c.1900; value: £200–250.** A good-quality gold fob chain is still a sound commercial object. Women often buy them to wear around the neck or wound round the wrist as a bracelet. This is a good example with nice curb links; value very much depends on weight and condition.

▲ **American shelf or wall clock, c.1890; value: £50.** Many of these American clocks were exported to Britain during the mid- to late 19th century, and most have yet to acquire any great value. This steeple model has a 30-hour movement, but those fitted with eight-day movements can be worth as much as £150 in good condition. For the most part they were manufactured by a number of companies in Connecticut, where production rose from a few thousand a year around 1840 to at least 8,000 a day by 1900, as wooden movements were replaced by inexpensive rolled brass. Dials are painted tin or even paper. Desirable makers include Seth Thomas, Chauncey Jerome & Co, W L Gilbert and the Welch Clock Company.

▲ **Ansonia clock, c.1900; value: £250–300.** The Ansonia company of Connecticut produced great quantities of these inexpensive mantel clocks with onyx cases, in imitation of much more impressive and more valuable French clocks of the same period. Many find their way to the *Roadshow*, although not usually in such good condition as this one.

Toys and dolls

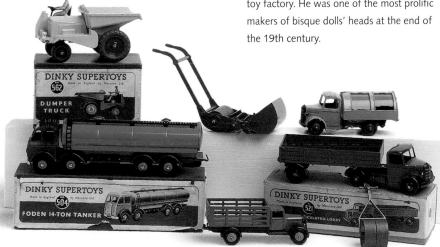

◀ **Armand Marseille AM 390 doll, c.1915–20; value: £250–300.** Doll experts working on the Miscellaneous tables see several of these dolls at every *Roadshow*. The Armand Marseille AM 390 was made in great numbers from 1915. Normally they are worth £120–200, but this is of better quality than usual, having detailed rather than line eyebrows. Armand Marseille, who worked between 1885 and 1930, was born in Russia but moved to Germany, where he set up a toy factory. He was one of the most prolific makers of bisque dolls' heads at the end of the 19th century.

▲ **Hornby Dublo electric train set, 1954; value: £200–300.** Many a small boy unwrapped one of these on a Christmas or birthday morning between 1938 and 1964. Meccano Ltd launched the Hornby Dublo range of clockwork and electric train sets in 1938. The number of sets such as this one that are brought to the *Roadshow* is a measure of how successful the range was.

▼ **Black doll, 1950s; value: £20–30.** Made by Pedigree, celluloid black dolls often turn up on the *Roadshow*. They began to be made in quantities in the 1950s, reflecting the period when West Indians first settled in Britain in considerable numbers.

▲ **Selection of Dinky vehicles, 1940s and 1950s; value: from £10 for the garden roller to £250 for the blue Foden tanker.** This smart collection of Dinky Supertoys, many with their boxes intact, has been much more carefully played with than the well-loved – in other words, rather battered – Dinky toys that are usually laid before the *Roadshow*'s toy experts. Dinky toys were launched by Frank Hornby in 1931 to accompany his railway series. They became one of the most popular toys ever to be produced in Britain, and remained world leaders until well into the 1960s. The blue tanker without its box and in a more typically worn condition would be worth £20–30.

Japonaiserie

In 1854 Japan began trading with the West once again after a long period of self-imposed isolation. It found a ready market in Europe for its decorative wares, which included metalwork and textiles as well as affordable pottery and porcelain.

Made specifically for export, many of these objects were shipped to the West in huge quantities, finding their way into so many British homes that they turn up in great quantity at every *Roadshow*. They were also brought back to Britain as souvenirs by sailors and others who travelled in the Far East. Because so many examples of *Japonaiserie* survive in good condition, values at the moment remain low. They are worth taking care of, as no doubt their day will come.

◀ Japanese fan, c.1930; value: £5–10. Textiles were exported from Japan well into the 20th century. This fan has ebonized and silvered guards, sticks made from wood, and a leaf of lace and woven silk painted with prunus blossom.

▲ Pair of bronze vases, c.1890; value: £40–50. They may look like brass, but these vases are bronze; the bright, shiny look is the result of regular polishing. However, if the original mellow tones of the metal are left alone to develop an attractive patina, the value may rise to £100–150.

▶ Japanese Kutani coffee pot and cup and saucer, c.1900; value: coffee pot £20–30, teacup and saucer £5. This is classic export ware, with the handle and spout of the coffee pot modelled on bamboo. It is known as eggshell porcelain because it is so thinly potted, and, if you're lucky, you'll find a lithophane of a geisha girl in the bases of cups or bowls.

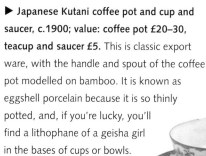

▲ Satsuma vase and cover, c.1910; value: £40–60. Made in moulds, rapidly hand-decorated and exported by the shipload at the turn of the 20th century, Satsuma vases and covers such as this are typically painted in iron red and gilt.

◀ Japanese eggshell porcelain coffee set, c.1930; value: £40 for the set. Hand-painted to depict samurai, coffee sets such as this one were bought in great numbers in Britain from the late 19th century until the Second World War.

Militaria

▲ **Christmas tin, 1914; value: £10–50 for the empty tin, up to £100 if complete with pencil.** These embossed gilt-metal tins were sent by Princess Mary, for Christmas 1914, to every soldier serving at the Front. They contained chocolate, cigarettes, a pencil, a signed photograph of the Princess and a Christmas card. Value depends on how many of the components are still intact.

▼ **Sword bayonet, 1910; value: £30–35.** Thousands of 1842-pattern sword bayonets for the French military rifle were imported from the Continent before the First World War by an entrepreneur who bought a stockpile of them left over from the Franco-Prussian War of 1870.

▲ **First World War medals, 1914–16; value: £35–50, depending on rank and obscurity of regiment.** Known as Pip, Squeak and Wilfred after cartoon characters featured in the *Daily Mirror*, these medals regularly turn up at the *Roadshow*. Servicemen who joined up in 1914–15 received the bronze Star as well as the silver War Medal and the bronze Victory Medal embossed with the angel; those who joined up after 1915 received the last two.

Glass

▼ **Enamelled glass jug, c.1850; value: £30–40.** Coloured glass enamelled in white (known as 'Mary Gregory') was made by every glassworks in England, as well as in Bohemia (now part of the Czech Republic), at this time. These jugs are common in green, red, blue and amethyst.

Fakes

▲ **Fake Art Deco figures, modern; value: £10–20.** The experts have become used to seeing fakes such as these at the *Roadshow*. Made in resin and stone, they imitate the expensive ivory and bronze figures that were produced towards the beginning of the 20th century by sought-after designers such as

Ferdinand Preiss (see page 95) and Demêtre Chiparus. The genuine article has always been desirable, giving rise to cheaper contemporary copies in spelter and alabaster. Objects thought to be ivory, but which are in fact made from resin, are among the most common causes of disappointment for *Roadshow* visitors.

The new collectables

The world of antiques and collecting is notoriously volatile. It is hardly surprising, therefore, that during the two decades that the *Antiques Roadshow* has been running, completely new areas of collecting have sprung up. Many of these were either unheard of or in their infancy when the programme was first broadcast.

In fact, 21 years ago an object had to be at least 100 years old to be taken seriously. The world of collectables, as opposed to antiques, was waiting to be discovered. At the beginning of the 1980s the spending power of a new generation of collectors – whose tastes and aspirations differed from those of their parents – forced dealers and auction-house experts to get to grips with entirely new markets.

French and German bisque-headed dolls, 19th-century automata and early tinplate toys were already being treated seriously, but, as the decade went on, modern toys began to rise in value. The young adults who had grown up in the 1950s and 1960s were beginning to buy the memorabilia of their childhood, and not just the toys. Anything related to the culture of the period was desirable, and this included printed ephemera, textiles, glass, plastics and ceramics.

Who would have thought then that teddy bears would make thousands of pounds at auction, or that rock and roll memorabilia would become attractive to so many collectors? As these items rose in value, the price of objects made earlier in the 20th century also increased. The field is now so wide and varied that it's not possible to cover it comprehensively, but here are a few of the things that, 21 years ago, might have been gently and politely dismissed by a *Roadshow* expert.

▼ **Writing desk by Heal & Son, London, 1928; value £3,000.** Heal & Son, which is still thriving today, began trading in the early 19th century. Ambrose Heal designed all the furniture for his family firm from 1896 until the 1950s. This writing desk in limed oak was made to order and sold as part of a limited-edition. It bridged the gap between very exclusive hand-made furniture and the inexpensive Art Deco furniture being mass-produced during the 1920s and 1930s. There is now a great deal of interest among collectors in the plain, clean lines of early Heal's furniture in limed and weathered oak.

▲ **Beatles bubble-gum machine, 1960s; value £150–200.** Rock and pop music have always made a lot of money for the stars and executives in the industry. However, it was not until the beginning of the 1980s that the first auctions of rock and pop memorabilia were held, and items from records and musical instruments to costumes and autographs began to fetch high prices. Beatles memorabilia is more valuable than that relating to any other icons of pop music. In the United States, coin-operated bubble-gum machines such as the example shown here featured a reproduction signed photograph of the Fab Four in an attempt to capitalize on the group's popularity.

▼ **Chad Valley mohair plush teddy bear, c.1935; value £400–600.** The first important auction of teddy bears was held at Sotheby's in 1983, and the market has gone from strength to strength. In December 1994 'Teddy Girl', made in 1904 by a German company, Steiff, sold at Christie's for a world-record price of £110,000. This one was made by Chad Valley, a leading toy manufacturer named after the district of Birmingham in which it was originally based.

▲ **Star Wars figures, 1990s; value £5–300 each.** Justin Pressland, seen here with a young collector at one of the children's *Roadshows*, describes *Star Wars* memorabilia as the most inter-generational collectables of the 20th century, appealing to young and old alike. The film *Star Wars* was released in 1977; the toys hit the market in 1978 and have been collected avidly ever since. Look out for figures still in their original packaging.

▶ **Shelley tea service, 1928–30; value £300–500.** Customers who unwrapped a Shelley tea service at the first series of the *Roadshow* in 1979 were politely told that they should 'use it and enjoy it': the time-honoured way of telling an owner that something is not worth a great deal. The reaction is somewhat different today, because this complete service is now very desirable. The Queen Anne shape is decorated in a Blue Iris design, hand-painted in enamels on a transfer-printed outline.

Glossary

Anchor escapement A type of escape mechanism (shaped like an anchor) on a timepiece. The anchor permits the use of a pendulum (either long or short) and offers greater accuracy than the verge escapement.

Applied decoration Surface ornament made separately and applied to the body of an object.

Aquatint A tonal etching simulating the effect of a watercolour.

Art Deco The first truly modern style to make full use of mechanized production and new materials. The term, which applies to interwar design, derives from L'Exposition Internationale des Arts Décoratifs et Industriels Modernes, the first major exhibition of the decorative arts held after the First World War, in 1925.

Art Nouveau Short-lived and excessive style that flourished between c.1880 and 1914. Characterized by curving, swirling organic forms and the whiplash motif.

Arte povera A decorative process in which prints are stuck onto a piece and then painted and lacquered.

Automata Moving figures operated by a mechanical device; mainly produced by clock makers in the 19th century.

Backplate a) With the frontplate, one of the two vertically aligned plates between which a clock movement is supported. b) The metal plate on to which a handle on a piece of furniture is mounted.

Balance wheel escapement A type of escape mechanism on a timepiece consisting of an oscillating wheel mounted above a movement that controls the going of a clock. Used on clocks that do not have a pendulum.

Banding Small sections or strips of veneer used around the edges of drawer fronts and surfaces on furniture to complement the principal veneer.

Baroque A highly ornate and extravagant style that sprang from the architecture of 17th-century Italy.

Barrel The cylindrical brass box containing the mainspring on a spring-driven clock. On a weight-driven clock, the line on which the weight is hung is wound around the barrel.

Blank A completely undecorated piece of pottery or porcelain.

Bombé Bulbous, curving shape particularly favoured in Continental Europe for commodes and other types of case furniture.

Body The material from which a piece of pottery or porcelain is made.

Bone china A type of porcelain containing 25 per cent china stone, 25 per cent china clay and 50 per cent ground calcined cattle bones. Produced extensively in England from the early 19th century and still made today.

Bonheur du jour A small lady's writing desk, originally made in France c.1760, with shelves or pigeon-holes at the back of the table surface.

Bracket clocks A portable clock, made in England from the late 17th century, designed to sit on a bracket fixed to the wall or on a table.

Britannia metal A type of pewter containing a high proportion of tin and often silver-plated, used to make an extensive range of goods in the 19th century.

Cabriole legs An elongated 'S'-shape leg on furniture, often with a pronounced 'knee'.

Caddy top Convex shape used on the top of many early longcase and bracket clocks.

Calf binding A type of smooth, polished-leather binding for books made from calfskin.

Cameo A shell or piece of hardstone cut to create a design in relief.

Carat A unit for measuring the weight of gemstones or the fineness of gold. In the case of gold, based on 24 units.

Carcass The main body of a piece of furniture before veneers are applied or doors, shelves or drawers are added.

Cellaret A deep, lockable box used for storing wine and first made during the 18th century. Either free-standing or incorporated into a sideboard in the form of a lead-lined drawer.

Chasing A method of decorating the surface of silver or other metal objects by indenting it, usually with a hammer and punches, to create patterns without removing any metal.

Chinoiserie Chinese-style decoration or objects made in the Chinese style in the 17th and 18th centuries.

Chromolithograph A commercial style of colour-printed lithograph common from the late 19th century.

Cloisonné Enamel decoration in which a network of metal wires is fixed on to the body of a piece; the resulting cloisons (compartments) are filled with coloured enamel paste before being fired.

Commode The French word for a low chest of drawers made from the mid-17th century onwards. The term is also used to describe a bedroom cupboard incorporating a chamber pot or washbasin.

Console A flat-sided bracket or corbel used, usually in a pair, to support a wall-fixed or free-standing table.

Crazing The fine network of cracks on a glazed surface caused by a different rates of contraction between the body and the glaze during firing in the kiln or because of an extreme change in temperature.

Davenport A small writing desk with a hinged top above a case of side drawers.

Delft Tin-glazed earthenware, named after the Dutch town where it was first made in the late 16th century. The term is also used to describe the wares of this type made in England.

Demi-lune A half-moon shape, usually applied to semicircular console tables.

Dial-plate On clocks, the metal plate to which the chapter ring and spandrels are attached.

Drop-leaf A table with hinged flaps that can be raised.

Dumb waiter A piece of dining-room furniture introduced c.1725 and consisting of a central stand supporting two or three tiers of circular trays.

Enamelling A method of decorating metal objects such as boxes with one or more layers of translucent enamels made from powdered glass to which metallic oxide pigments are added to give colour.

Engraving A method of decorating metal or glass by cutting into the surface with a sharp tool or revolving copper wheels.

Embossing A method of producing a design in relief by hammering on the reverse side of an object.

Escapement The part of a clock that controls the speed at which it runs, thereby regulating its timekeeping.

Etching A type of printing where the image is drawn on to a metal plate covered in wax. The plate is submerged into a bath of acid that eats into the surface of the plate, following the drawn image.

Expressionism A style of painting in which the artist seeks to express emotional experience rather than impressions of the external world.

Famille rose Chinese porcelain painted in a palette that is predominantly an opaque rose-pink enamel.

Feathering A decorative effect resembling the fine lines of a feather, created by moving coloured glazes while still wet on ceramic bodies with a fine tool.

Foxing Brownish stains on works on paper caused by mould and exposure to damp air.

Fresco A painting done in watercolour on a wall or ceiling while the new plaster is wet.

Frieze The framework immediately below a table top or a decorative panel of sculpture or ornament.

Frontispiece The illustration facing the title page of a book.

Genre painting Scenes of everyday domestic life or anecdotal subjects with a literary, sentimental or historical theme.

Gesso A type of plaster made from powdered chalk and size that lends itself to being carved, painted or gilded. Used extensively on picture frames and for detailed relief work on furniture.

Gilding The technique of decorating glass, ceramics, furniture or picture frames with gold leaf, gold dust or gold paint.

Glasgow Boys/School An informal brotherhood of artists in late-19th-century Glasgow who rebelled against the Scottish artistic establishment.

Glaze The glass-like coating of varying colour, thickness and opacity that renders ceramic objects impervious to liquids.

Gothic Revival The 18th- and 19th-century revivals of the medieval style that flourished between the 11th and 15th centuries. Characterized by slender, soaring lines and the pointed arch, rib vault and flying buttress.

Hallmarks The complete set of stamps put on to a piece of silver or gold to designate its standard of purity and date.

Hard-paste porcelain A type of porcelain body made using kaolin and petuntse, first developed in China. Also referred to as 'true porcelain'.

Hardstone The term used to describe opaque stones and semiprecious gems such as agate, cornelian, onyx and bloodstone.

Incised decoration Decoration that is cut into the body of an object with a sharp metal point.

Inlay A design usually cut from veneers, metal or mother-of-pearl and set into the surface of an object to decorate it.

Impressionism A style or movement in art concerned with expression of feeling by visual impression, exploiting especially the effect of light on objects.

Intaglio The process of carving or engraving in a hard material.

Kneehole desk A desk made in one section with a central recessed cupboard below the frieze drawer and three drawers either side.

Kutani Ceramic wares made in the Kutani region of Japan from the 17th until the early 20th centuries and including the widely exported eggshell teawares.

Lithography A process of producing prints from a stone or metal surface that is treated so that the image to be printed can be inked while the remaining areas reject the ink.

Lithophane Thin translucent porcelain panels or plaques that when held to the light reveal pictures or designs that seem three-dimensional. Usually made of unglazed biscuit porcelain, and sometimes moulded into the bases of cups, mugs and other hollowares.

Longcase clocks A tall, narrow clock with a base that sits on the floor. Also known as a grandfather clock.

Lopers A pull-out support to hold up the fall front of a bureau or the drop-leaf of a table.

Marcasite A yellowish crystal iron-sulphide mineral used in jewellery making.

Marquetry An ornamental pattern on the surface of an object that is created by laying together shaped pieces of coloured veneers, or slivers of tortoiseshell, ivory, mother-of-pearl or metals.

'Mary Gregory' glass The name given to coloured glass decorated in opaque white enamel with scenes of Victorian children at play, made and exported from Bohemia to the United States, where, it is said, they were copied by a Mary Gregory working at the Boston and Sandwich Glassworks.

Medium The material used by a craftsman or artist in creating an object or work of art.

Ming porcelain The wares produced during the dynasty that ruled China from 1368 to 1644.

Minute repeater *See* Repeater.

Mother-of-pearl The inner lining of shells of molluscs such as oyster, nautilus and abalone.

Movement The mechanism of a clock, usually made of brass with some steel parts. Early American clocks were often made with wooden plats and wheels, and wood was also used in German, Swiss and Austrian clocks.

Neo-classical A style that dominated Europe during the late 18th century, inspired by the architecture and ornament of ancient Greece and Rome following the excavations at Herculaneum and Pompeii.

Netsuke A Japanese toggle, often extremely decorative and carved from wood or ivory, worn at the waist above the *obi* (sash). Once part of traditional Japanese costume, they fell out of use as Japanese men adopted Western dress in the late 19th century.

Obelisk A tapering, four-sided pillar with a pyramidal point usually made from stone or marble, set up as a monument or landmark, but also made in smaller sizes as decorative objects.

Objects of virtu An antiques term meaning 'precious objects', used to describe small, luxury pieces in silver, gold, porcelain or enamel, such as seals, *bonbonnières* and snuff-boxes, etuis and needlecases, often decorated with gilding or precious gems.

Ormolu Bronze that has been gilded with an amalgam of mercury and gold. Such a piece was then fired to drive off the mercury, leaving the gold adhering to the bronze.

Orrery A model of the planetary system or planetarium, often with a clockwork or hand-cranked mechanism, that was used as a piece of astronomical demonstration apparatus in the 18th and 19th centuries.

Overglaze decoration A process applied to ceramic bodies using enamel paints to decorate an object after it has been glazed. The piece is then returned to the kiln to fuse the enamels on the glazed surface.

Palladian A Classical architectural style inspired by the 16th-century Italian architect Andrea Palladio that greatly influenced 18th-century English furniture designers such as William Kent.

Paris School The coterie of foreign artists who lived and worked in Paris during the early part of the 20th century and greatly influenced the direction of European art.

Patina The changes on the surface of an object, whether wood, bronze or silver, as the result of the passage of time. Good patination, which is impossible to fake, raises the value of a piece; destroying it by cleaning lowers value.

Pembroke table A small table with two drop-leaves and one or more drawers beneath the centre section, said to have been introduced by the Countess of Pembroke, who ordered the design in the 18th century.

Pier table A small side table designed to stand against the 'pier', which is the wall between two windows.

Pierced decoration A decorative effect on wood, porcelain or metal created by cutting through the surface to form a pattern.

Plique à jour **enamel** A type of enamelling in which wire is soldered on to a metal base to form cells which are then filled with translucent coloured enamels. After firing, the base is dissolved and a coloured, glass-like shell remains. The appearance is similar to stained glass.

Porcelain *See* Soft-paste porcelain and Hard-paste porcelain.

Provenance The known history of an object, including records of previous owners.

Regency The term for the style prevalent in England between 1800 and 1830, named after the Prince Regent, later George IV.

Relief decoration Decoration that stands out from the surface of an object and is usually described, according to its depth, as low- or high-relief.

Renaissance The period in European art and literature from the late 14th to the early 17th century which revived the ideals of Classicism.

Repeater A clock or watch in which the user pulls a cord, depresses a lever or presses a button to make it repeat the strike for the last hour or quarter-hour. Clocks or watches that repeat the last five minutes are rare.

Rococo A decorative style that flourished particularly in France between 1720 and 1760, characterized by asymmetrical 'C' and 'S' scrolls and the rockwork (rocaille) inspired by Chinese garden design.

Rolled gold A form of plating in which thin sheets of gold are fused to base metal and then rolled out to form a sheet. This method is used extensively in the manufacture of inexpensive jewellery.

Salt-glazed stoneware A stoneware piece covered with a thin, clear glaze produced by throwing a handful of salt into the kiln during firing.

Salver A flattish tray or dish.

Satsuma ware Cream-coloured Japanese earthenware covered with a yellowish glaze, densely painted and richly gilded, named after the port of Satsuma, but made in various parts of Japan.

Seconds dial A small dial on a clock or watch calibrated in seconds.

Sgraffito A decorative technique in which the surface of an object (usually ceramic) is scored to reveal the darker colour beneath; the word in Italian means 'scratched'.

Shibayama The Japanese technique of inlaying an object with a combination of mother-of-pearl, ivory and stones to create a pattern or scene surrounded by lacquer.

Slip Liquid clay.

Slipware Ceramic wares decorated with slip.

Soft-paste porcelain A mixture of clay, powdered glass and other materials, including bone ash, flint and sometimes soap stone, that was developed by 18th-century European potters while trying to imitate true porcelain produced in China and Japan. It is also known as 'artificial porcelain'.

Spandrels The triangular corner spaces between an arch or circle and a rectangle. In a clock, the ornamental corners between the chapter ring and the dial-plate.

Table-cut diamond One that has been cut to create a flat, table-like surface.

Transfer printing A method of transferring a design created on a copper plate via transfer paper on to a pottery or porcelain body.

Underglaze decoration Decoration applied to a ceramic body before glazing and final firing.

Veneer Thin layers of fine wood such as mahogany, rosewood and satinwood applied to a carcass of much coarser wood.

Verge escapement A type of escape mechanism on a timepiece. The verge escapement, which is driven by a pendulum (usually short and bulbous), is more accurate than the balance wheel escapement.

Watercolour A painting created by using water-based paint.

Whieldon-type wares Mottled, lead-glazed wares in tortoiseshell, greens and yellows that are named after the English potter Thomas Whieldon (1719–95).

Index

Page numbers in *italics* refer to picture captions.

A
Ablott, Richard 107
Adam, James 90
Adam, Robert 90
Adam style 90
Adam, William 90
Aesthetic movement 45
agateware 105
Allderidge, Patricia 96
Allum, Marc 21, *21*
Ancients, The 97
Ansonia *142*
Archdale, George 21, *21*
Archdale, Sonia 47
arms and armour
  experts 24, 29
  see also militaria
Art Deco 22, 95, *95*, 145
Arts and Crafts movement *42*, 59
Ashford 125, 133
Atterbury, Paul 22, *61*, 71, 87, 117
Atterbury, Zoe 80
auction house open days ('sweeps') 10
Audemar, Jules-Louis 121
Audemar Piguet 121, *121*
autographs *81*
automaton by Gustave Vichy 134, *134*
Axford, John 21, *21*

B
Baddeley, Jon 21, *21*
BAFTA award 83
Baker, Keith 23, *23*, 67
Bandini, Rosemary 23, *23*, 68
Banwell, Tony 23, *23*, 128
Barnstaple 96
Battie, David 18, 25, *25*, 78, 105-6, 117
BBC Bristol 10, 50, *50*
Beilby, Mary 108
Beilby, William 108, *108*
Belfast 81
Belgium 74, 76
Benjamin, John 23, 23
Benson, W A S 42
Bérain, Jean 89
Bent 120
Berlin factory 106, *106*
Berwick-on-Tweed 93
Bestell, Alfred 79
Bett, Hugh 24, *24*, 127
Bexhill-on-Sea 95, 118
Bibles *139*
Biddlecombe, John 56, 57
Bienaimé, Luigi, *The Arming of Telemachus* 94, *94*
Bing 137
bird cages *36*
Bishop, Andy 55
bisque *140*, *143*
Blake, William 97
Blenheim Palace 126
Bly, John 28, 88, 91, 92
Bognor Regis 134
Böhme, Karl Wilhelm 106
Bolton 127
Bone, John 50, 52, 53, *54*, 58, 74
bonheur du jour 28, 93
books and manuscripts 25, 79, 138, *139*
  experts 24, 27, 35
  great finds 125-7
Borghese family 109
Borrmann, Johann Balthasar 106
Bowers, Birdie 127
Bowett, Adam 24, *24*, *60*
bracket clocks 119, *119*

Brazier, Dave 63, 69, 79, *80*
Bridlington 135
Bristol 81
Brittain, Penny 31, *31*, *60*, *64*, 111
Britannia metal *141*
bronze 95, 114
Brussels 115
Bugatti, Carlo *61*, 87
Bull, Simon 18, 32, *32*, 63, 109, 120-1
Burges, William 117, *117*
Burgess, Michèle 50, *51*, 62, 69
Burlington, Richard Boyle, 3rd Earl 89
Burne-Jones, Edward, *King Cophetua and the Beggar Maid* 42
Butler, Roy 24, *24*, 129, 130

C
cabinet makers, 18th-century 88
Calvert, Edward 97
cameras and camera crews 54, 56, 57, 62, 65, 69, 70
  camera tests 63
  macro 62
  portable single-camera unit ('PSC') 56, *68*
  scanner 52, 62, 69, 79
Campione, Bunny 36, *36*, *64*, 68, 79, 133, 135
Canova, Antonio 94
Cardiff 81
Carette 137
Carrara marble 94, *94*
Carroll, Lewis 126, *126*
cartes de visite 139
cartoons 82, 83-4
Cartwright, Peter 53
Cary, John and William 122, 123
celluloid 95, 137, *143*
ceramics
  great finds 101-7
  see also pottery and porcelain
Chad Valley 135, *135*, 147
Chatsworth 116, 137
Chauncey Jerome & Co *142*
Chelsea factory 111
Cheltenham 131
Chepstow 104
children's *Roadshows* 78, *78-81*, 128, 147
Chiparus, Demêtre 95, *145*
choosing pieces for filming 62, 66
chromolithographs *138*
chryselephantine 95
Clarke, Stephen 24, *24*
Cleethorpes 62, 91
Cleman, Edward 113
Clement, William 118
clocks and watches 62, *142*
  experts 24, 37, 40
  great finds 118-21
cloisonné 114, *114*
close-ups and details *see* cutaways
Clwyd 114
Cobb, John 88
Cochran, C B 95
Colchester 89
Colinet 95
collectables 35, 39, 40, 78, 79, 138-47
Collectors' World 10, 19, 37
Collingridge, James 26, *26*, 65, 114
Collins, David 26, *26*
commemorative items *140*
commode, English marquetry 88, *88*
Cook, Captain James 125
Cooper, Margie 26, *26*, 63
coral 113, *113*
cornelians 109
costume 132, *132*
Crawley 112
creamware 105, *105*
cross-over ring *140*
Curry, John *64*
cutaways 62, 72

D
Dadd, Richard 96
  Artists Halt in the Desert 96, *96*
Darlington 122
Davenport 93
Davenport factory 107, *107*
Davis, Andrew 26, *26*
De la Portas 109
demi-lune tables 90, *90*
Denmark 74, 76
Derby factory 107
desks
  bonheur du jour 28, 93
  Davenport 93
  kneehole 93, *93*
diamonds 115-16, *115*, *116*
Dickenson, Alastair 27, *27*
Dinky *80*, *143*
directors 62, 72, 79
Disney figures 135-6, *135*, *136*
dolls *see* toys and dolls
Doulton Lambeth 22
Drake, Robin 11, 18, 19
drawings *see* pictures and prints
dumb waiters 28, 92, *92*
Durham, Sir Philip 129
Dutch cabinet makers 88
Dwight, John 102, *102*

E
Eaton Hall, Chester 94
ebony 109
Edinburgh 81
editing 62, 72, 72, 73
  cutaways (close-ups) 62, 72
  layback 72, 73
  paper edit 72, *72*
  sound 72, 73
electroplating *141*
embroidery 131-2, *131*, *132*
enamel
  cloisonné 114, *114*
  on glass 108, *108*, 145
  Mughal gold bracelets 115, *115*
Enniskillen 92
ephemera 138, *138*, *139*
Euclid, The First Six Books of the Elements of 25, *25*
experts 17, 18, 20-47, 67

F
Fabergé, Carl 116, *116*
fakes 79, 95, 145
Farahar, Clive 27, *27*, 79, 125, 126
Farahar, Sophie 47
Farnham 109
Farquharson, Sir Joseph 45
feathering 90, 103
Fidler, Amanda *51*
Fitzalan Howard, Josephine 27, *27*
Forrester, Philippa *81*
Foujita, Tsuguharu (Leonard) 100, *100*
France 74, 76
Frederick the Great 106
Frodsham 120
Fromanteel, Ahasuettis 118
Frost, Pat 27, *27*
Fry, Elizabeth 110
furniture 28, *28*, 36, *64*
  condition reports *60*
  experts 24, 33, 38, 41
  furniture round 58, *58-61*
  great finds 88-93
  transporting 58, *59*, *60*

G
general views ('GVs') 56
German cabinet makers 88
Gibraltar 74, 76, 76
Gilbert, W L *142*
Glasgow Boys (Glasgow School) 99, *99*
glass *145*
  great finds 108
globes, library 122, *122*

Godden, Geoffrey 29, *29*, 107
Going for a Song 10, 37
Going Live 78
gold *120*, *130*, *140*
  great finds 109, 113, 115
Golitsin, Prince 94
Gothic Revival *42*, 117, *117*
Greene, Sarah 78
Gubelin Lucerne 121
Guer, G 22

H
Hamblen, Stan 55
Harper, John 79
Harriman, Bill 29, *29*
Harris, Ian 29, *29*, *80*, 113
Harris, Natalie 29, *29*, 47, *80*
Hay, Jane 30, *30*
Heal's *22*, *146*
Hemel Hempstead 90
Hereford 10-11, 12, 18, 19
Herrengrund 30
Hinds-Howell, Rosamund 30, *30*, 47
Hogarth, *The Harlot's Progress* 46
Hooke, Robert 118
Hook, Philip 18, 30, *30*, 100
Hornby *143*
Hornel, Edward Atkinson 99, *99*
Horsham 106
Hudson, John 30, *30*
Huguenot craftsmen 88, 116
Humphries, Barry 55
Hunt & Roskell 112
Hunter, Storr and Mortimer *11*
Huygens, Christiaan 118

I
ice pail *25*
Ince, William 90
Inglis, Brand 33, *33*, 111
Inverness 98
Ipswich 129
Isle of Man 88
Islington 100
Ivers, Glenn 55
ivory 95, 97, 114, *145*

J
Jamaica 74, 76, 77
Japanese bronze and silver elephant 114, *114*
Japonaiserie 144, *144*
jewellery 62, 75, *140*
  experts 23, 29
  great finds 115-16
Johnson, Joseph and Alfred 135
Jones, Nikki 50, *50*
Jones, W & S 123, *123*

K
kadas 115, *115*
Kakiemon *11*
Kay, Hilary 39, *39*, *64*, 71, 78, 81, 123, 124, 132, 134, 136, 137
Kent-style table 89, *89*
Kent, William 89
Kevill-Davis, Sally 33, *33*
kneehole desks 93, *93*
Knowles, Eric 33, *33*, *81*, 95
Kulberg, Victor 120

L
Lambert, Deborah 33, *33*, 88
Lang, Gordon 34, *34*, 102
Langlois, Pierre (Peter Langley) 88
layback 72, 73
Lay, Graham 21, 34, *34*
Lealand, Peter 124
Leatham, Victoria 34, *34*, 102, 131
Lewis, Christopher 20, 50, *50*, *51*, 52, 55, 58, 60, 62, 72, 74, 82, 83
lighting 52, 52-4, 57, 65
Linnel, John 90
Linnel, William 90
lithography 138
Liverpool 105

Lloyd's Patriotic Fund 129
   sword 129, *129*
local helpers 55, *63*
locations 12-15
   children's *Roadshows* 81
   local views 67
   overseas 74, *74-7*, 76
Lockett, Terence 34, *34*, 107
longcase clocks 118, *118*
London 81, 128
Looker, Rob 53, *55*
Lowestoft factory 25, 104, *104*
Lowry, L S 22
Lozano, José Honorato 74, 76
Lynas, Frances 35, *35*

M
Maas, Rupert 35, *35*, 67
macro 62
Malta 74, *74*, *75*, 76
Manchester 81
manuscripts *see* books and
   manuscripts
Maria Federovna, Tsarina 115
Märklin 137, *137*
marquetry commode 88, *88*
Marseille, Armand *143*
Marsh, Hugo 35, *35*, *79*, 80
Marvel, Chris *31*
May, Ada 95
Mayhew, John 90
medals, military 130, *130*, *145*
Medici family 109
Meiji Period (Japan) 114
Meissen 106
Merry, Elizabeth 35, *35*
metalwork *141*
   see also arms and armour; gold; silver
Meyer, Friedrich Elias 106
Michelham Priory 120, 130
Mickey Mouse, tinplate 136, *136*
microphones 66
microscope 124, *124*
Midleton, Alan 37, *37*
militaria *145*
   great finds 129-30
   see also arms and armour
Mills, Nathaniel 112
Ming dynasty porcelain 101, *101*
miniature by George Richmond 97, *97*
Minton 22
miscellaneous experts 21, 23-4, 26,
   30, 33-4, 37-8, 41, 43-4, 47
Mitchell, Nicholas 37, *37*, *58-61*
Moorcroft 22, *22*
Moreton-in-Marsh 136
Morley-Fletcher, Hugo 10, 18, 37, *37*
Morris, Barbara 37, *37*
Motherwell 99
Mughal dynasty 115
Munn, Geoffrey 42, *42*, *79*, 116
Murphy, H G 22
music, opening sequence 73

N
Nahum, Peter 38, *38*, *60*, *76*, 96-8
Neal, John 50, 52, *52*, *53*, 74
Negus, Arthur 10, *10*, 18, *19*, 134
Neo-classical style 90, *90*, 94
Nero's Golden House 89
Netherlands 74, 76
netsuke 114
Newcastle Emlyn 108
Newman, Michael 38, *38*
Newton, John 110
Nicol, Liz 50, *51*
Nielsen, Nicholas 120
'noddies' 62
Northampton 103

O
objects of virtu 28
   great finds 117
Olive, Steve 73

opening sequence 67, 72, 73
orrery 123, *123*
overseas locations 74, *74-7*, 76
Ozzy the Owl 103, *103*

P
painted furniture 91, *91*
paintings
   great finds 96-100
   see also pictures and prints
Palladian style 89
Palladio, Andrea 89
Palmer, Samuel 97
Paris School 100
Parker, Bruce 18, *18*
Parker, Kevin 55
pattens 132
Payne, Christopher 38, *38*, 90
Pearson, Sebastian 38, *38*
Peebles 115
Pembroke table, painted 91, *91*
Peninsular War 130
Philippe, Patek 121
Philips, Sir Thomas 96
photographs 126-7, *139*
Pickford, Ian 40, *40*, 110, 112
pictures and prints 67, 74, 76, 138, *138*
   experts 26-7, 30, 35, 38, 40, 43, 47
   see also paintings
pieces to camera ('PTCs') 56
pier tables 90
Piguet, Eduard-Auguste 121
Piper, John 22
planning 50
pocket watches 120, *120*, *142*
Poltimore, Mark 40, *40*
Ponting, Herbert 127
Poole Pottery 22
Poole, Trevor 55
porcelain *see* pottery and porcelain
portable single-camera ('PSC') 56, 68
postcards *139*
Potter, Steve *51*, 73
pottery and porcelain *64*, 140
   experts 21, 23, 29, 30, 33-5, 37-8,
   41, 43-4
   see also ceramics
Japonaiserie 144, *144*
Powell & Lealand 124, *124*
Powell, Hugh 124
Powell, Thomas 124
Poynter, Sir Edward 42
Preiss, Ferdinand 95, *95*, *145*
presenters 18-19
   children's *Roadshows* 78, 81
Pressland, Justin 40, *40*, *79*, *147*
Price, Richard 40, *40*, 118, 119
prints *see* pictures and prints
public 62, *62*, 69
Pugin, Augustus Welby Northmore 22
punch pot 105, *105*

R
rattle 113, *113*
Rawlings, Charles 113, *113*
reception experts 47
recording dates 12-15
Renaissance 89
   gold plaque 109, *109*
Richmond, George, 97
   In the First Garden 97, *97*
Rippon, Angela 18-19, *18*
Rochdale 113
Rockingham 107
Rock, Orlando 41, *41*
rock and pop memorabilia 65, 78, *146*
Ronner, Henrietta 98, *98*
Roscoe, Barley 41, *41*, 47
Rouse, James 107
Rowley, John 123
Rundell, Bridge & Rundell 111, 129
Rupert Bear 79
Russian silver pendant 115, *115*
Rylands, James 41, *41*

S
St Helier 97
Salisbury 111
salt cellars *11*, 110, 111, *111*
salt-glazed stoneware 102, *102*
Sandon, Henry 45, *45*, 69, 103
Sandon, John 41, *41*, 65, 108
scanner 52, 62, 69, 79
Schofield, Phillip 78
Science Museum 128
scientific instruments 39, *39*
   great finds 122-4
Scott, Deborah 47
Scott, Robert Falcon 127, *127*
Scully, Hugh 17, 19, *19*, 57, 66, 75,
   78, *81*, 82, 83
   closing broadcast 70
   introduction 56, *56*, 57, 67
   opening sequence 67, 72, 73
sculpture
   great finds 94-5
   19th-century Italian 94, *94*
Senior, Chris 57, *70*
set
   design and construction 50, 52,
   52-5, 58, 61, 74
   dismantling 71
Sèvres 22
sgraffito 103, *103*
shagreen 110
Shelley *147*
Sheraton 28
shibayama 114
shoes, 18th-century silk 132, *132*
shop, souvenir 52, 70
silver *11*, 22, 28, 62, *80*, *142*
   experts 24, 26-7, 33, 40, 44
   great finds 110-15
silver-plate *141*
Skegness 117
slipware 103, *103*
Smallwood, Karen 51
Smith, Pete *51*, 57, 67, 70
Smith, Richard 57
Smith, S, & Son 120
Snow White doll 135, *135*
snuffbox, porcelain 106, *106*
soft-paste porcelain 104
Somerville, Stephen 43, *43*
sound and sound engineers 56, 65,
   66, 67, 70, 71
   crowd noise 71, 72
   editing 72, 73
   layback 72, 73
   voice-overs 56, 67
spelter *141*
Spencer, Chris 43, *43*, 104
spinet *11*
Sprimont, Nicholas 111
Stafford 123
Staffordshire slipware 103, *103*
stamps
   experts 23
   great finds 128
Star Wars memorabilia *147*
Steele, Thomas 107
Steiff *147*
Stewart-Lockhart, Clive 43, *43*, *81*
Stinton, Harry 45
stirrup cups 112
Stoke-on-Trent 124
Storr, Paul 111, *111*
Stowmarket 121
Summers, William 113, *113*
Sweden 74, 76
Sweet, John 55

T
tables
   Neo-classical demi-lune 90, *90*
   Pembroke 91, *91*
   William Kent-style 89, *89*
Talking about Antiques 19

Taubenheim, Philip 43, *43*, 47, *80*
Taylor, Kerry 44, *44*
Taylor, Samuel 110, *110*
tea caddies 110, *110*
technical design 50, 52
teddy bears 36, *147*
Teed, Richard 129
television operatives ('TVOs') 52,
   53, 62
textiles
   experts 27
   great finds 131-2
Tharp, Lars 46, *46*, 64, 67, 101
Thomas, Seth *142*
Thompson, Robert 'Mouseman' 22
Thorvaldsen, Bertel 94
Thunderbirds 80
tinplate toys 136-7, *136*, *137*
Tipp & Co 136, *136*
toastmaster's glass 108, *108*
tortoiseshell ware 105
tourbillon mechanism 120
toys and dolls 35, 36, 39, *39*, 40,
   79, 80, *143*
   great finds 133-7
toys and collectables experts
   35, 40
Trafalgar, Battle of 129
train sets *143*
transport team 58, *59*, 60
Treacher, Clive 55
Tufin, Sally 22

U
Ullmann, Philip 136

V
Vacheron & Constantin 121
venues 12-15, 50
Vichy, Gustav 134, *134*
Vichy, Henri 134
Vienna Secession 99
Vile, William 88
Viney, Paul 44, *44*
vision desk 69
voice-overs 56, 67

W
Waddesdon Manor 101
Wade 45
Waldron, Peter 44, *44*
walnut veneer kneehole desk
   93, *93*
Walsall 102
watch chains *142*
Watson-West, Sally 47
Weekin clockwork toys 135
Welch Clock Company *142*
Wellings, Norah 135
Wellington 107
Wellington, Arthur Wellesley,
   1st Duke 106
Weymouth 119
Whieldon, Thomas 105
Whieldon-type wares 105, *105*
White, Cliff 69
White, Debbie 69
Wilson, Joshua 118
Windermere 132
wine bowl 112
Wirral 94, 116
Wonnacott, Tim 44, *44*, 68, 71
Wood, Christopher 47, *47*
Wood, John 55
Wood, Steve 72
Worcester factory 25, 45, *45*
Wright, Vincent 72
Wyndham, Henry 47, *47*, 99

Y
Yeovilton 110
Yirrell, Alec 47, *47*, 52, 55, 62,
   63, 70, 80
Yirrell, Christine 47
York 81

Author acknowledgements

Thanks are due to the following for their generous help in the preparation of this book:
Christopher Lewis, Adèle McGeorge, Tony Hunt, Michèle Burgess, Clive Corless and Jill Churchill.
Special thanks go to Tim, Kitty and Freddie Marlborough for their patience and support.

Picture acknowledgements

Key

Reed Consumer Books Limited: **RCB**; Tim Ridley: **TR**;
Clive Corless: **CC**; Marshall Editions Developments: **MED**;
Nick Goodall: **NG**; Christie's Images: **CI**; Sotheby's London: **SL**.

Front cover RCB/TR; **back jacket c** CC/Frederick Warne & Co; **back jacket t** RCB/TR; **back jacket bl** CC; **back jacket br** SL; **1** City of Stoke on Trent Department of Leisure and Cultural Services. City Museum and Art Gallery/Photos courtesy of Potteries Museum and Art Gallery, Stoke-on-Trent (formerly the City Museum and Art Gallery, Stoke-on-Trent); **2** RCB/TR; **5** CC; **7** RCB/Ron Sutherland; **8-9** BBC Picture Archives and Photograph Library; **10** BBC Picture Archives and Photograph Library; **11t** MED/CC; **11c** CC; **11bl** CC; **11br** CC; **12t** RCB/TR; **12b** RCB/TR; **13t** RCB/TR; **13b** RCB/TR; **14t** RCB/TR; **14b** RCB/TR; **15** RCB/TR; **16-17** RCB/TR; **18l** The BBC, Bristol; **18r** BBC Picture Archives and Photograph Library; **19t** BBC Picture Archives and Photograph Library; **19b** BBC Picture Archives and Photograph Library; **20** RCB/TR; **21tl** CC; **21tr** CC; **21bl** CC; **21br** SL; **22t** RCB/TR; **22b** RCB/TR; **23tl** CC; **23tr** CC; **23bl** CC; **23br** CC; **24tl** CC; **24tr** CC; **24bl** CC; **24br** CC; **25t** RCB/TR; **25b** RCB/TR; **26tl** CC; **26tr** CC; **26bl** CC; **26br** CC; **27tl** CC; **27tr** CC; **27bl** CC; **27br** CC; **28t** RCB/TR; **28b** RCB/TR; **29tl** CC; **29tr** CC; **29bl** CC; **29br** CC; **30tl** CC; **30tr** CC; **30bl** CC; **30br** CC; **31t** RCB/TR; **31b** RCB/TR; **32t** RCB/TR; **32cr** RCB/TR; **33tl** CC; **33tr** CC; **33bl** CC; **33br** CC; **34tl** CC; **34tr** CC; **34bl** CC; **34br** CC; **35tl** CC; **35tr** CC; **35bl** CC; **35br** CC; **36t** RCB/TR; **36b** RCB/TR; **37tl** CC; **37tr** CC; **37bl** CC; **37br** CC; **38tl** CC; **38tr** CC; **38bl** CC; **38br** CC; **39t** RCB/TR; **39b** RCB/TR; **40tl** CC; **40tr** CC; **40bl** CC; **40br** CC; **41tl** CC; **41tr** CC; **41bl** CC; **41br** CC; **42t** RCB/TR; **42b** RCB/TR; **43tl** CC; **43tr** CC; **43bl** CC; **43br** CC; **44tl** CC; **44tr** CC; **44bl** CC; **44br** CC; **45t** RCB/TR; **45b** RCB/TR; **46t** RCB/TR; **46b** RCB/TR; **47tl** CC; **47tr** CC; **47b** CC; **48-49** RCB/TR; **50 left** RCB/NG; **50 right** RCB/NG; **50c** RCB/NG; **51tl** RCB/NG; **51tr** RCB/NG; **51c** RCB/NG; **51b** RCB/NG; **52 left** RCB/TR; **52 right** RCB/TR; **52c** RCB/TR; **53tl** RCB/TR; **53tc** RCB/TR; **53tr** RCB/TR; **53bl** RCB/TR; **53bc** RCB/TR; **53br** RCB/TR; **54tl** RCB/TR; **54tr** RCB/TR; **54b** RCB/TR; **55tl** RCB/TR; **55tr** RCB/TR; **55b** RCB/TR; **55bl** RCB/TR; **56r** RCB/TR; **56tl** RCB/TR; **56bl** RCB/TR; **57tl** RCB/TR; **57tr** RCB/TR; **57cl** RCB/TR; **57bl** RCB/TR; **57br** RCB/TR; **58l** RCB/TR; **58r** RCB/TR; **59tl** RCB/TR; **59tr** RCB/TR; **59bl** RCB/TR; **59br** RCB/TR; **60tl** RCB/TR; **60tr** RCB/TR; **60c** RCB/TR; **60b** RCB/TR; **61t** RCB/TR; **61c** RCB/TR; **61b** RCB/TR; **62l** RCB/TR; **62r** RCB/TR; **63tl** RCB/TR; **63tr** RCB/TR; **63cl** RCB/TR; **63cr** RCB/TR; **63bl** RCB/TR; **63br** RCB/TR; **64tl** RCB/TR; **64tr** RCB/TR; **64cl** RCB/TR; **64c** RCB/TR; **64b** RCB/TR; **65tl** RCB/TR; **65tr** RCB/TR; **65c** RCB/TR; **65b** RCB/TR; **66tl** RCB/TR; **66tr** RCB/TR; **66c** RCB/TR; **66bl** RCB/TR; **66br** RCB/TR; **67tl** RCB/TR; **67tr** RCB/TR; **67cl** RCB/TR; **67cr** RCB/TR; **67b** RCB/TR; **68tl** RCB/TR; **68tr** RCB/TR; **68c** RCB/TR; **68b** RCB/TR; **69tl** RCB/TR; **69tr** RCB/TR; **69bl** RCB/TR; **69br** RCB/TR; **70tl** RCB/TR; **70tr** RCB/TR; **70c** RCB/TR; **70b** RCB/TR; **71tl** RCB/TR; **71tr** RCB/TR; **71bl** RCB/TR; **71br** RCB/TR; **72 left** RCB/TR; **72 right** RCB/TR; **72cr** RCB/TR; **73t** RCB/TR; **73cl** RCB/TR; **73b** RCB/TR; **74** CC; **75t** CC; **75bl** CC; **75br** CC; **76t** CC; **76c** CC; **76b** CC; **77t** Brian Hawkins; **77b** Brian Hawkins; **78t** RCB/NG; **78bl** RCB/NG; **78br** RCB/NG; **79tl** RCB/NG; **79tr** RCB/NG; **79c** RCB/NG; **79bl** RCB/NG; **79br** RCB/NG; **80tl** RCB/NG; **80tr** RCB/NG; **80cl** RCB/NG; **80cr** RCB/NG; **80bl** RCB/NG; **80br** RCB/NG; **81t** RCB/NG; **81cl** RCB/NG; **81cr** RCB/NG; **81b** RCB/NG; **82** CC; **83tl** Jonathan Pugh/*The Times*; **83tr** Ben Shilow; **83c** *Private Eye*/Berkin; **83b** Peter Knight/AUGUSTA Copyright cartoon by permission of Angus McGill and Dominic Poelsma; **84t** Bellworks/Steve Bell; **84c** *The Spectator*/Reproduced from *The Spectator*; **84bl** Mirror Group Newspapers/Langdon; **84br** *Radio Times*/Ken Pyne; **85t** RCB/TR; **85b** Jennifer Birkby; **86-87** RCB/TR; **88** The BBC, Bristol; **89** MED/CC; **90** MED/CC; **91** MED/CC; **92** CC; **93** CC/N Brand; **94** CC; **95** CC; **96** BBC Picture Archives and Photograph Library; **97** CC; **98** CC; **99** CC; **100** CC; **101** CC; **102** CC; **103** City of Stoke-on-Trent Department of Leisure and Cultural Services. City Museum and Art Gallery/Photograph courtesy of the Potteries Museum and Art Gallery, Stoke-on-Trent (formerly the City Museum and Art Gallery, Stoke-on-Trent); **104** CC; **105** SL; **106** CC; **107** CC; **108** CC; **109** MED/CC; **110** CC; **111** The Salters Company; **112t** CC; **112b** CI; **113t** CI; **113b** CC/N Brand; **114** MED/CC; **115t** *BBC Homes and Antiques* magazine/CC; **115b** CC; **116tl** CC; **116tr** CC; **116b** CC; **117** CC; **118** The BBC, Bristol; **119** CC; **120l** CC; **120r** CC; **121** CC; **122** MED/CC; **123** MED/CC; **124** CC; **125tl** CC; **125tr** CC; **126t** CC; **126c** CC; **126b** CC; **127tl** CC; **127tr** CC; **128** SL/Sotheby's Hong Kong; **129** Lloyd's; **130l** *BBC Homes and Antiques* magazine/CC; **130r** *BBC Homes and Antiques* magazine/CC; **131l** CC; **131r** CC; **132** CC; **133** CC; **134** SL; **135** CC/©Disney; **136t** CI/©Disney; **136b** CI/©Disney; **137** Devonshire Collection, Chatsworth/Reproduced by permission of the Chatsworth Settlement Trustees; **138bl** CC; **138br** CC; **139tl** Paul Atterbury; **139tr** CC; **139cl** Paul Atterbury; **139cr** Paul Atterbury; **139bl** CC; **139br** CC; **140tl** CC; **140tc** CC; **140tr** CC; **140cl** CC; **140cr** CC; **140bl** CC; **140br** CC; **141tl** CC; **141tr** CC; **141b** CC; **142tl** CC; **142tc** CC; **142tr** CC; **142b** CC; **143tl** CC; **143tr** CC; **143bl** CC; **143br** CC; **144tl** CC; **144tr** CC; **144cl** CC; **144cr** CC; **144b** CC; **145tl** CC; **145tr** CC; **145c** CC; **145bl** CC; **145br** CC; **146t** RCB/Ian Booth; **146b** RCB/Pro-Photo; **147t** BBC Picture Archives and Photograph Library; **147c** RCB/Sue Pearson; **147b** CC.